THE MUSIC COPYRIGHT MANUAL

THE MUSIC COPYRIGHT MANUAL

The Definitive Guide to Music Copyright Law in the Digital Age

JIM JESSE

To Ann, Sean and Paul

ACKNOWLEDGMENTS

Thanks to my wife, Ann Jesse, for her diligent proof-reading and editing of this book. Writing is editing, and she caught a lot of things. I want to give a shout out to Emma Reaney for designing a great cover and to her mom, Ann Reaney, for taking my photo. Thank you also to KU law students Maggie Turek, Lucas Homer and Baylee Suskin, who at various times helped do legal research for me on all the various topics. Maggie was particularly helpful in doing some editing and legal suggestions. Lastly, a bow to Kerry Altenbernd at the Douglas County Law Library where I often wrote and researched for this book.

PRAISE FOR ROCK N ROLL LAW SEMINARS

"If all CLEs were this good, lawyers would spend all their time in the classroom."

-Chris Mason, Oregon attorney

"I've been to over a hundred CLE Seminars in my 40 years' of practice, but never enjoyed one as much as yesterday's in Orlando. Thank you for the smart and hilarious presentation, especially about The Beatles. John, Paul & George are heroes of mine."

-Lamar Oxford, Florida attorney

"A+! We got the steak, not just the sizzle."

-Edward J. Tucker, New Jersey attorney

"Least boring CLE ever! Any CLE that plays clips and music from *Seinfeld* and *The Big Lebowski* is ok by me."

– Colleen Schaller, Pennsylvania attorney

"Not only is the presentation fun and entertaining, but I learned much more about the fundamentals of copyright law than I anticipated. Great CLE and well worth the time."

-Ron Pritchard, Kansas City attorney

"Very interesting and entertaining. A nuts and bolts primer for the non-copyright practitioner who wants to expand his knowledge of the law. This course contributed to my knowledge and love of music and its history."

-Larry Schaffer, Kansas City attorney

"I represent a recording studio and several artists and writers. This CLE was right on par with the work I do. It was both entertaining and informative! Thank you."

-Melanie D. Bingham, Kansas attorney

"Jim's CLE presentations are the best I have ever attended in over 40 years of practicing law. Jim knows his stuff and makes everything interesting for the audience."

-Bob Hiller, Kansas attorney

"With most clients' online and social interests, knowledge of copyright law is critical. In this age of internet and social networking, your clients will have copyright issues. This class is excellent."

-Henry Cox, Kansas City attorney

"I have an ownership interest in a recording studio and wanted to learn more about the business side of the music industry. I expect to revisit these materials often and plan to change our business model based on lessons learned in Jim's presentation."

-Gary Miller, Florida attorney

"This was my 4th time coming to a Rock N Roll Law seminar. I already had my CLE requirements for the year but came because it is so much fun."

-Jeff Zimmerman, Kansas City attorney

"Jim is knowledgeable and clearly lives the subject matter."

-Joe Ferrante, Ohio attorney

TABLE OF CONTENTS

PREFACE

I love music, write songs and am a lawyer. This book combines all those elements. I want to tell you what this book is not about. It does not concentrate on all of Music Law. It concentrates on Music Copyright Law, though if you know about copyrights, you know most of music law. I do not dwell much on touring, management, merchandising, or aspects of being a musician that do not relate to the songs. For that, I advise you get the latest version of Donald Passman's excellent *All You Need to Know About the Music Business*.

While I describe the book as the definitive guide to music copyright law in the digital age, it does not mean that it is the definitive guide on every topic. This book is meant to give the practitioner a framework from which to analyze these issues and dig deeper when needed. Topics such as fair use, public performance, and infringement could be discussed in an entire book of their own, along with many of the other topics in this book. I did not want to get too much into the weeds, but to give you the tools and resources needed to dive down if you so wish.

This book has been years in the making, as I travel the country spreading the gospel of Rock N Roll Law. I hope you enjoy, learn and take something from it.

SECTION ONE

● ● ●

INTRODUCTION TO MUSIC COPYRIGHT PRINCIPLES

Chapter 1

● ● ●

A "BITTERSWEET" STORY OR "WHY IT'S IMPORTANT TO KNOW ABOUT THIS STUFF"

In 1965, the Rolling Stones had a hit with the song "The Last Time" from their album *Out of Our Heads*. Their first manager (and producer) was Andrew Loog Oldham. A couple of years later, he did an orchestral version of the song. Last I checked, you can listen to it on YouTube.

In the mid-90's the British rock group The Verve landed a huge hit with their song "Bittersweet Symphony." The song's main hook was based on the string section of Oldham's song. The song's lyrics were written by The Verve's vocalist Richard Ashcroft. Originally, The Verve had negotiated a license to use a sample from the Oldham recording with his record label, Decca. As documented in Fred Goodman's recent biography of music business manager Allen Klein, who died in 2009, the rights to the composition and recording were both owned by ABKCO, Klein's company. Hence, ABKCO was the U.S. publisher for The Stones' song "The Last Time" as well as much of their material from the '60s and early '70s. The Verve had failed to contact ABKCO prior to "Bittersweet's release.

Klein was a ruthless negotiator who made it a personal mission to win any dispute. He was also very litigious, having been involved in approximately 40 lawsuits over his career. Klein also had the upper hand because the song had already been released and was a huge hit before The Verve retroactively sought a license from ABKCO. "We were told it was going to be a 50/50 split, and then they saw how well the record was doing," says band member Simon Jones. "They rung up and said, 'We want 100 percent or take it out of the shops, you don't have much choice.'" While Ashcroft is listed as a co-author for writing the lyrics to the song, he was paid a paltry $1,000 to transfer them to ABKCO. After shaking down The Verve, Klein told a friend, "I was very bad today."

After losing the composer credits to the song, Richard Ashcroft commented, "This is the best song Jagger and Richards have written in 20 years," noting it was their biggest U.K. hit since "Brown Sugar." Ashcroft is quoted as saying that "despite all the legal angles and the bullshit, strip down to the chords, the lyrics and the melody, you realize there is such a good song there."

In a 'Cash for Questions' interview with Q magazine published in January 1999, Keith Richards was asked if he thought it was harsh taking all The Verve's royalties from "Bittersweet Symphony," to which he replied, "I'm out of whack here, this is serious lawyer shit. If The Verve can write a better song, they can keep the money."

There are many ironies to this story. The two biggest are these. First, The Stones' influence for their song is a tune by The Staple Singers called "This May Be the Last Time." The Stones' song sounds so much like the Staples' song that I have seen it on a list of the best Stones' covers of all time even though the Staples' song came out ten years before The Stones' tune. By the way, you generally cannot copyright a song title—many songs have the same or similar titles. The second irony is that the string riff The Verve used from the Oldman composition sounds nothing like The Stones' song, and was written by the arranger David Whitaker, who was never even given credit for it. We will revisit this case later, but it illustrates the importance that songwriters and musicians (or their attorneys) know the basics of music copyright law and get the necessary permissions before a song is released.

Chapter 2

● ● ●

A BAND IS A BUSINESS

A Band or Artist is a business and should be treated as such. Yes, it is fun and likely not an artist's source of income or job, but if you plan to publicly release music, sell your music, or play live, then you should do three things. If you're in a band, have an operating agreement, set up a corporate entity, and establish a tax structure.

Setting Up a Corporate Entity

I am not a corporate expert, but in most states, a limited liability company (LLC), or something to that effect, is the simplest corporate structure. As the name implies, it will shield your personal assets from the corporate (band) debts. LLCs are easy to set up and there is minimal paperwork. Usually, you just file a form to rent it every year. Bands are not going to have corporate structures, a board of directors, meetings and minutes. With an LLC, you do not need any of that.

As we will see, copyrights initially vest with the author of a work, but there is a distinct difference between the author and the owner of a work. A band's corporate entity can own the band's songs via its publishing company, and its sound recordings via its own record label, for example. Even solo artists should do this.

Setting Yourself Up as a Tax Entity

Most musicians do not make a profit, let only much money, but if you set up yourself or your band as a tax entity, you can write off (deduct) reasonable business expenses. Being a musician can be expensive, particularly if you tour or have a home recording studio. Write off drums, speakers, or recording equipment. Now, I am not a tax expert either, so consult one if necessary to find out what tax entity works best for you, such as a sole proprietor, Sub S Corporation, or a partnership.

Have an Operating Agreement

Most bands will not do this, except successful ones, but it is important to have a basic understanding of how money is to be split and the band is to be run before money comes in. This is especially important for bands because there are multiple people involved. I will give some topics to be covered, but this list is not exhaustive, and there are no correct answers to these topics. Every band situation is different. I just want to present some topics to think about.

Who are the leaders of the band? Is it one-person, one-vote? Is there a tie-breaker for an even number of band members? Rarely are all members of a band truly equal. Whoever founded the band may think they are the leader. In my observation, it is typically the songwriters who assume the leadership role because they create the band's product. The leaders of The Stones are Mick and Keith. The Beatles were John and Paul. The Eagles were Don Henley and Glen Frey. In all those cases, they were the principal songwriters. I cannot think of any band where the main songwriter is not one of the leaders.

Who gets the composing credit? To get songwriting credit, your contribution must be more than minor and creative (not just funding a project). Now this is not a clear line. So, contributing a word or two may not warrant credit, but a whole line might. One chord or basic chord changes might not rise to songwriting credit, but a unique chord structure or guitar riff may. Again, this needs to be worked out before because the composer in a band has access to revenue streams that the others do not. In some bands, it will be clear who the main composer is, while in others, it may be more of a group effort.

There is a scene in The Go-Go's *Behind the Music*, where the drummer calls the accountant and asks how much money each member of band made. The songwriters (Charlotte Caffey and Jane Wiedlin) made a lot more than the others, and the drummer was livid. The band called a meeting, and the writers were asked to split all songwriting royalties equally among the band. When they refused, the band broke up for 17 years. There can also be agreements between co-writers about splitting song royalties.

Who is the Author/Owner of the Sound Recordings?

I will flesh out what sound recordings are in a bit, but this can be a more complex question because more goes into how a song sounds. The composition is the lyrics and melody, but the sound recording (master) comprises the production, performances, and everything that goes into a song's sound. Now, if you are recording all by yourself in your home studio, it is easy to say who the author is. But a whole band contributing to a song is quite different, especially if you throw in a producer. The simplest thing is to have the entire band own the master (assuming you do not transfer it to a record company).

Who owns the band name? Is it the group's LLC? Axl Rose and Mike Love ended up owning the names Guns n' Roses and The Beach Boys, respectively.

How are members added or removed? This is not something you want to think about, but it often comes up in bands.

How are other revenues such as touring and merchandise to be split? A band is a brand and who owns it? Do you have a logo that has been trademarked?

Chapter 3

● ● ●

ORIGINS OF COPYRIGHT LAW, DURATION AND PUBLIC DOMAIN

The framers of the US Constitution stated that "Congress has the power to promote the Progress of Science and useful Arts, by securing for limited Times to Authors and Inventors the exclusive Right to their respective Writings and Discoveries." While music is not explicitly stated, we shall see that it is included in the definition of a copyright. Indeed, most creative endeavors as we know them, did not exist at the drafting of the Constitution.

Why do we have copyrights? Because a great nation deserves great Art. We want creators to benefit from their creations. Copyrights act as an incentive to create. If everyone could just take your work and make money from it, you may not have as much incentive to create. As the Supreme Court has explained, "[b]y establishing a marketable right to the use of one's expression, copyright supplies the economic incentive to create and disseminate ideas." The purpose of copyright law is to advance a culture of creativity, which the government believes benefits society at large; otherwise, what's the incentive to create if everyone owns it? Plus, it is a new nation without any art or culture to speak of.

I do not spend a lot of time in this book on history unless it is particularly relevant to the law today. The main thing to gather from the Constitution quote above is that this is strictly a Federal area of law. Prior to the major copyright revisions that took effect in1978, there were state and common copyright laws, so if you are dealing with an old recording or song, that may come into play. I do not talk much about that though because it does not affect music made today, or for the last 40 years. As such, while there may be differences among federal, district and circuit courts, you do not have all 50 states weighing in. All the statutory authority on copyrights is found in Title 17 of the U.S. Code.

Public Domain

There are songs whose copyrights have expired, or they existed prior to modern copyright laws. Those songs are in the "public domain." This means anyone can use or cover those songs without getting permission or paying money. Most works enter the public domain because of old age, like old folk songs or most classical music.

Here's how songs enter the public domain:

1. Song published in the U.S. prior to 1923;
2. Songs published before 1964 which were not renewed before 1978;
3. Songs published without a copyright notice, which was required prior to March 1, 1989;
4. Creator just wanted to give the song/work away.

Note that if you gathered songs from the public domain into a collection, they may, as a whole, be protected as a collective work, and most likely as a sound recording.

Practice Tip: Make sure all of a song is really in the public domain before using or recording it.

You can waive your copyright in any work, in whole or part. Creative Commons is a non-profit organization that allows creators to dedicate their work to the public domain after they created it, or after a certain period of time. Be careful with a work that has multiple copyrights, because some of the work may be in public domain, while other parts are not. For example, a song can be in the public domain, while the sound recording may not; or, a movie is in the public domain, but the soundtrack (songs) are protected. Further, if you modify, or add to, a public domain work, that modification may be copyrightable. Go to www.creativecommons.org for more info.

Practice Tip: We will discuss licensing later, but if you want to use another's music, you could avoid expense and time, by licensing or using a song from Creative Commons than traditional methods.

How Long Copyrights Last

For all songs published after 1977, the copyright lasts for the author's life, plus 70 years. That period runs until the end of the calendar year, so if the songwriter dies on January 1, 2018, the work is protected until December 31, 2088. If there is more than one author, the 70 years does not begin to run until the last author dies. They last 70 years after an author's death in order for the author's heirs to benefit from, and direct the use of, the copyright they have inherited. Copyrights are personal property, so state laws regarding that do apply. As such, they can be transferred, given away, assigned, and bequeathed.

The term of copyright protection of a work made for hire is 95 years from the date of publication or 120 years from the date of creation, whichever expires first.

The Act accords a special scheme to joint works. "In the case of a joint work prepared by two or more authors who did not work-for-hire, the copyright endures for a term consisting of the life of the last surviving author and 70 years after such last surviving author's death." Thus, to determine the duration of a joint work copyright, it is necessary to be aware of the identity of all the joint authors, as well as the dates of their respective deaths, and to measure years from the death of the last survivor. If there are several authors of a given work, that computation may be difficult. That the term of protection for joint works is calculated from the death of the last surviving joint author makes it advantageous for an older author to choose a younger one as collaborator. Indeed, it even suggests that some works that would otherwise be written by a single author will become joint works, solely in order to measure the term of protection upon the life of a younger "joint author." Of course, this result will not be achieved if it can be proven that the relationship of joint authorship was not bona fide.

Chapter 4

● ● ●

WHAT IS A COPYRIGHT AND WHAT CAN BE COPYRIGHTED?

"Copyright" is the term used to describe several legal rights that exist in original literary, musical, dramatic or artistic works, and in sound recordings, films, broadcasts and other creative works. Under copyright laws, these rights are exclusive to the copyright owner or author, and enable the copyright owner to control how their work is used and to prevent unauthorized use. Copyright is a "limited duration monopoly." Given the broad language in the Constitution, it was up to Congress to define what a copyright is exactly. 17 U.S.C. 102 defines what is protected by copyright law.

> "(a) Copyright protection subsists, in accordance with this title, in original works of authorship fixed in any tangible medium of expression, now known or later developed, from which they can be perceived, reproduced, or otherwise communicated, either directly or with the aid of a machine or device. Works of authorship include the following categories:
>
> (1) Literary works;
>
> (2) Musical works, including any accompanying words;
>
> (3) Dramatic works, including any accompanying music;
>
> (4) Pantomimes and choreographic works;
>
> (5) Pictorial, graphic, and sculptural works;
>
> (6) Motion pictures and other audiovisual works;
>
> (7) Sound recordings; and

(8)   Architectural works.

(b)   In no case does copyright protection for an original work of authorship extend to any idea, procedure, process, system, method of operation, concept, principle, or discovery, regardless of the form in which
it is described, explained, illustrated, or embodied in such work."

The above list is meant to be illustrative and not exhaustive. For example, you
can copyright computer software code even though it is not explicitly on the
above list. Now, as it relates to music, you can copyright sheet music, which
is not listed above, although it certainly embodies music and lyrics. It would
likely fall under a literary work.

"The administrative classification of works has no significance with
respect to the subject matter of copyright or the exclusive rights provided by
this title." Under subsection (b) above, you cannot copyright a song's theme
or idea such as lost love, vindication, or any other common theme running
through popular music; otherwise, there would not be much to write about.
You do not have a monopoly on an idea.

Multiple Copyrights in a Single "Work"

Copyrights can exist in all sorts of things; for example, music, lyrics, pho-
tographs, artwork, books, speeches, TV programs, and movies. Also, what
might appear to be a single work can include several different copyrights
owned by several entities. In this digital multi-media age, it is very common
to have many different copyrights in it. Even something as simple as a book
can have several copyrights in it such as pictures, cover art, a CD or audio version. I recently saw a musical that I think included at least four copyrights: the
play itself (the performance if it was recorded), the musical compositions, the
sound recording (they were selling a CD of the songs), and the written words
of the play (the book). A music video is an audio-visual work that includes the
musical composition as played from a sound recording.

**Practice Tip: The more copyrights you have in a work, the more poten-
tial owners there are. This can create issues when the rights holders are**

not on the same page. So, it helps when the same person owns all of the copyright.

Here is a diagram of what started out as a book, and became multiple copyrights.

What is NOT Copyrightable?

Several categories of material are generally not eligible for federal copyright protection. These include, among others:

* songs that have not been fixed in a tangible form of expression. An example would be any song that has not been written or recorded (e.g. it's only in your head). Of course, if they are just in your head there's nothing tangible to copyright;

* titles, names, short phrases, and slogans, familiar symbols or designs, mere variations of typographic ornamentation, lettering, or coloring

and mere listings of ingredients or contents. So, you cannot copyright a song title—there are several songs with the same title— "I Love You" or "Love is a Wonderful Thing." Now, if a song has a REALLY unique song title, it is possible to get a trademark for it;

* ideas, procedures, methods, systems, processes, concepts, principles, discoveries, or devices, as distinguished from a description, explanation, or illustration. So, you cannot copyright a song idea of "getting your heart broken" or "redemption." You can only copyright the song itself;

* works consisting entirely of information that is common property and containing no original authorship (for example: standard calendars, height and weight charts, tape measures and rulers, and lists or tables taken from public documents or other common sources); as it relates to music, for example, a list of notes, music scales, common chords or chord changes.

What Can Be Copyrighted?

All works are eligible for copyright protection if they are "original" and "fixed in a tangible form." I will address these in turn.

ORIGINALITY

Originality has a low threshold. A work is "original" if it owes its origin to the author and was not a result of copying. The work does not need to be novel or unique in any way. Originality for copyright purposes amounts to "little more than a prohibition of actual copying. No matter how poor the author's' addition, it is enough if it be his own." Although slavish copying involving no artistic skill whatsoever does not qualify, a showing of virtually any independent creativity will do.

To be copyrightable, a song must be original and of "sufficient materiality" to constitute a work. "Close Encounters of the 3rd Kind" (5 notes) and the NBC chimes at the top of the hour (three notes) are examples of what can be copyrighted. Courts have said that a song consists of rhythm, harmony, and melody, and there must be creativity in at least one of the three. Some courts say it is impossible to copyright a rhythm, while others have found an "uh-oh" in a distinctive rhythm to be copyrightable. Courts have found creativity in fingering, dynamic marks, tempo indications, phrasing, and guitar licks.

Courts have been reluctant to give harmony, by itself, copyright protection, probably because it is dependent on the underlying melody. Thus, the melody (and lyrics) is the usual source of protection for musical compositions. Now, all songs bear some similarity to prior ones—i.e. all music is derivative. But, originality only requires that you created it independently and that the overall impression is of a new work. But occasionally, Courts will declare something not original as they did in *Newton v. Diamond*. In that case, a judge found that the Beastie Boys' use of a 3-note sample, where they had permission to use the sound recording but not the music itself, was permissible because the sample was not original and the use was de minimis. It should be noted that the sample was only six seconds of their song "Pass the Mic," although it was used at the very beginning of the song, and it was also only a 3-note phrase that used just two notes.

FIXATION

For a work to be "fixed," its embodiment in a copy or phonorecord must be "sufficiently permanent or stable to permit it to be perceived, reproduced, or otherwise communicated for a period of more than transitory duration." [1]

"It makes no difference what the form, manner, or medium of fixation may be--whether it is in words, . . . notes, sounds, . . . and whether it is capable of perception directly or by means of any machine or device 'now known or later developed.'" After all, there could be means of recording and listening to music that no one has thought of yet. Certainly, technology on how to record and listen to music has rapidly changed over the years. In my life, the music industry has gone from 45s and 8-track tapes, to albums, to cassettes, to CDs, to downloads and now streaming. Most music today is created on, or even by, computers; thus, music on your hard drive is fixed in a "tangible medium of expression."

---

1 Alcatel USA, Inc. v. DGI Techs., Inc., 166 F.3d 772, 787 (5th Cir. 1999).

Chapter 5

● ● ●

THE TWO COPYRIGHTS IN EVERY SONG

If you remember anything from this book, please remember there are two copyrights in every recorded song. They are: a © which stands for "Copyright" and a (p), which stands for "Phonograph". Phonograph comes from the old machines that used to play vinyl records. If you look at liner notes to an album you may see both used. Another thing you need to know is that if an artist is on a major label, the label generally owns the sound recordings (or master), while if the artist is on their own, the artist will own it.

Copyright in the music and lyrics will usually be owned by the artist or their music publishing company, and copyright in the sound recording will usually be owned by the artist's record label. Use of that track, including any adaptation of the track or any uploading or sharing over the Internet, will require the permission of these copyright owners, either directly or through their representatives (for example, through a performing rights organization). We will flesh this out much more later.

So, to use the example from The Stones' song "The Last Time," Mick and Keith wrote the music, notes, melody and words, along with the lyrics. The actual recorded version of that song, i.e. how it sounds on the album *Out of Our Heads,* is another copyright. Thus, one song can have many different sound recordings such as a live version, demo, acoustic version, dance mix, alternate take, and so forth.

The "Two Worlds of Music" and What a Record Label Does

I am fairly certain that most of you have at least a general understanding of what a record label is and what they do. A record label is a company that markets music recordings and music videos. Often, a record label owns its own publishing company and the sound recording of its artists; coordinates the production, manufacture, distribution, marketing, promotion and enforcement of copyright for sound recordings and music videos; conducts talent scouting and development of new artists ("artists and repertoire" or "A&R"); and maintains contracts with recording artists and their managers.

One of the major developments in the music world over the last two decades is that indie artists can now perform all the functions that labels used to provide, and that the labels themselves do not even perform all the above tasks anymore. For example, major labels do not do much in the way of production because they will usually contract with someone for that. I do not think they have a lot of A&R people looking for new talent or are even interested in developing an artist.

The record contract controls the relationship between the label and the artist, and when an artist first signs with a label, they have no leverage and must sign whatever is put in front of them. The contract will tell the band how many albums they need to make in a certain period of time. In the 1960s, groups like The Beatles had to release two albums and two singles per year. The label will tell the artist when, and if, their albums are released, and control what songs are released as singles.

In the current music universe, there are two general worlds—the major record labels (Sony, Warner, and Universal) and their subsidiaries, and independent artists on their own. Now, there's certainly a continuum from major indie labels to small or boutique labels with one artist.

Practice Tip: If a musician creates and makes their own music, they are essentially their own record label. As such, they are responsible for everything in the definition of a record label above.

As stated above, in the major label world, the record label often owns the masters (the sound recording rights), while the songwriter owns the musical composition (the publishing). Certainly, one or the other may own a piece of either, but if both entities are not on the same page, this can create obstacles and opportunities. In the case of the indie or DIY world, the artist likely will own both copyrights. For a humorous and recent example of the nuances of two copyrights in each song, search "Def Leppard" on npr.org for their story on how the group got around their differences with their old record label by exploiting that there are two copyrights in a song.

Sound Recordings

Section 101 of the Copyright Act defines sound recordings as "works that result from the fixation of a series of musical, spoken, or other sounds, but not including the sounds accompanying a motion picture or other audiovisual work." Common examples include recordings of music, drama, or lectures. A sound recording, however, is not the same as a phonorecord. A phonorecord is the physical object in which works of authorship are embodied. The word "phonorecord" includes cassette tapes, CDs and vinyl discs as well as other formats such as music downloads. So, a sound recording is the song's sound fixed on a phonorecord. This copyright was created as of February 15, 1972. The reason for the creation was the rampant piracy of sound recordings. Sound recordings fixed before February 15, 1972, are not eligible for federal sound recording, but may fall under common or state copyright laws.

Sound recordings, in theory, are derivative works. While it is hard to think that a sound recording has "originality," it is comprised of many different things. First, a performance can certainly be original. Second, the author of a sound recording can be producer. A producer helps the artist record the song and enhance the songs and album as a whole. Congress acknowledged the contribution of "capturing and electronically processing the sounds." Thus, the plain text of the Copyright Act makes clear that reproduction occurs when a copyrighted work is fixed in a new material object.

"Phonorecords" are material objects embodying fixations of sounds such as cassette tapes, CDs, or vinyl discs. Thus, for example, a song can be fixed in sheet music ("copies") or on vinyl records ("phonorecords"), or both. If a work is prepared over a period of time, the part of the work that is fixed on a particular date constitutes the created work as of that date.

Two copyrights in every song

Song

Music/Lyrics

Sound Recording

You can also get a copyright in the arrangement of a song. This is done quite often in classical music and songs that have entered the public domain. It is possible to get this with a copyrighted work as well. To claim this, however, the arrangement must be original, and there appears to be a higher standard of originality if you just arranged it.

Sound recordings last for a flat 70 years because they are usually owned by an entity, such as a record label, so there is no life attached to it. In Europe, sound recordings that are not released after 50 years enter the public domain. So, if you have a Bob Dylan bootleg from his 1966 shows in London, and Dylan (Columbia Records) does not release it, you could. That is why Dylan, and a host of others to come, will be releasing entire tours' worth of music at once so the label, and not bootleggers, can make the money.

Who Is the Author of a Sound Recording?

Only those who made original contributions may claim ownership of a sound recording, or entities who get those interests assigned to them, such as record companies. Sound recordings, like motion pictures, can have many people contribute to the work, so the question of ownership can be complex. This can be solved via work-made-for-hire or assigning an interest in the work. I talk about works-made-for-hire later. Congress specifically left it up to the employment relationship and bargaining among the parties to hash this out. Certainly, the question of leverage is important here, and most people involved in a sound recording on a major record label will assign their interest in the work.

The relationship of a record producer to a band/artist is usually as an independent contractor. In the early days of rock music, producers like The Beatles' George Martin were in fact employees of the record label. Absent an assignment or employment relationship, which usually happens, the owner of a sound recording will either be the artist or a joint ownership between the artist and the producer. Jay Z was sued by a woman who came in and sang counter-melody on a track. There was no work-for-hire agreement, and there was no evidence he intended this to be a joint work, and she could not claim ownership over the whole song. The plaintiff was not successful in establishing authorship.

Chapter 6

●　●　●

HOW TO OBTAIN A COPYRIGHT

Under Section 102 of the Act, copyright protection lies in "any tangible medium of expression." Thus, the instant you write or record an original song so as to prove you created it, be it on a piece of paper (lyrics) or sing it into your iPhone--in other words, putting the intangible into tangible form-- you have created a copyright. So, once it is fixed in a tangible form, you have a copyright. You do not have to register it. Once a band or songwriter puts their songs on a cassette, burns it to a CD, or records it on a hard drive (how most music is created now), they have a copyright.

Fixation

A work is not "fixed" unless it is "sufficiently permanent or stable to permit it to be perceived, reproduced, or otherwise communicated for a period of more than transitory duration." Live events and radio are fixed if the fixation is taking place at the time the work is being made simultaneously with the transmission.

It should be noted that there is a difference between "original works of authorship" and the material objects which the work must embody in order to satisfy the fixation requirement. For example, sound recordings are "works of authorship" fixed in "phonorecords" which contain such sounds. As long as a song is fixed in any tangible medium of expression, regardless of the nature of such medium, it is no longer necessary that such medium be visibly intelligible. Thus, there is no need to put the song into sheet music form, and it is possible to copyright a song just by recording it, even if the composer does not reduce it to notes. Sound recordings can be fixed on a computer chip.

When is a work "created" so as to begin the term of statutory copyright? Section 101 provides: "A work is 'created' when it is fixed in a copy or phono-record for the first time. When a work is prepared over a period of time, the portion of it that has been fixed at any particular time constitutes the work as of that time; when the work has been prepared in different versions, each version constitutes a separate work. Because "creation" requires "fixation," and is not "fixed" unless it is embodied in a tangible medium of expression by or under the authority of the author, a work is not created for statutory copyright purposes if it is recorded, filmed, or otherwise embodied in tangible form solely by one who does so without the author's permission.

Why You Should Register Your Copyright

If you are going to attempt to make money, play live, or in any way commercially exploit your songs, even as a hobby, I recommend registering your songs with the Copyright office and through copyright.gov, specifically. Now you have a copyright prior to registering your song and/or sound recording because you must have something tangible to copyright, and copyrights exists when you have a "tangible medium of expression." Registering your song with the Copyright Office in Washington D.C. entitles you to more rights such as being able to sue over your copyright and the right to statutory damages and attorney fees. Copyright must be formally registered in the Register of Copyrights. Simply filing for registration does not meet the requirement. A copyright owner may file a lawsuit subsequent to registration for infringements occurring prior to registration.

Thus, if registration is made within three months after publication of the work or prior to an infringement of the work, statutory damages and attorney fees will be available to the copyright owner in court actions. Otherwise, only an award of actual damages and profits is available to the copyright owner, and there may be little or no actual damages. So, the remedies of statutory damages and attorney fees can only be obtained if registration occurs BEFORE the infringement. Registering your songs or sound recordings prior to infringement gives a potential plaintiff more leverage. I have represented plaintiffs who feel their song has been infringed. While they certainly have a copyright, they have not registered it with the Copyright Office. The defendant will find this out via discovery, and in cases where there are little, or no, actual damages, they will just say "buzz off" (or its legal equivalent). Statutory damages can be as high as $30,000, plus attorney fees. So, if you register, a plaintiff can hold that over the head of the defendant.

Publication is defined in the Copyright Act as "the distribution of copies or phonorecords of a work to the public by sale or other transfer of ownership, or by rental, lease, or lending. The offering to distribute copies or phonorecords to a group of persons for purposes of further distribution, public performance, or public display constitutes publication. A public performance or display of a work does not of itself constitute publication." Prior to 1978, publication and notice used to be a much bigger deal; such a big deal, in fact, that if you did not do one or the other correctly, you could lose your copyright. If you are dealing with a work from that era, tread carefully and make sure you have a valid copyright.

Five good reasons to register your song in the Copyright Office:

1. You can sue for copyright infringement.
2. You have access to statutory damages and attorney fees (leverage).
3. It acts as a public notice so if someone wants to pay you to license your song, they can more easily find you.
4. It may be a way for you to collect mechanical royalties from reproduction (discussed in next section).
5. It prevents someone else from falsely claiming authorship or ownership of your songs or sound recordings.

Who May File a Copyright Application Form?

The following persons are legally entitled to submit an application form:

* The author or authors. This is either the person who actually created the work or, if the work was made for hire, the employer or other person (or entity) for whom the work was prepared.

* The copyright claimant. The copyright claimant is defined in Copyright Office regulations as either the author of the work or a person or organization that has obtained ownership of all the rights under the copyright initially belonging to the author. This category includes a person or organization who has obtained by contract the right to claim legal title to the copyright in an application for copyright registration.

* The owner of exclusive right(s). Under the law, any of the exclusive rights that make up a copyright and any subdivision of them can be transferred and owned separately, even though the transfer may be limited in time or place of effect. The term "copyright owner" with respect to any one of the exclusive rights contained in a copyright refers to the owner of that particular right. Any owner of an exclusive right may apply for registration of a claim in the work.

* The duly authorized agent of such author, other copyright claimant, or owner of exclusive right(s). Any person authorized to act on behalf of the author, other copyright claimant, or owner of exclusive rights may apply for registration.

There is no requirement that applications be prepared or filed by an attorney. The fees to register a copyright are $85 for paper application and $55 for online (uploading it). You can register multiple songs as a compilation (album).

Can I register a collection of works with a single application?

A collection of works may be registered with a single application if either of the following requirements is met:

1. The collection is made up of unpublished works by the same author and owned by the same claimant; or
2. The collection is made up of multiple published works contained in the same unit of publication and owned by the same claimant.

Practice Tip: Register an entire album or group of songs together if the above two provisions are met. It's cheaper to do and gets you the same protection as registering all the songs separately.

Filling out the Proper Copyright Form

There are two copyrights in every song, so there are two potential forms to fill out.

Fill out Form SR (stands for sound recording) if you are the author or owner of the sound recording and/or the music composition.

Fill out Form PA (stands for performing arts) if you are the author or owner of the song.

Select Sound Recording if you are registering a sound recording. Also, select Sound Recording if you are registering both the sound recording and the underlying recorded musical, dramatic, or literary work(s), along with the sound recording of the work(s).

Note: To register both the sound recording and the underlying work on a single application, the copyright claimant must own all rights in both works.

Select Motion Picture/Audiovisual as the "Type of Work" for sounds accompanying an audiovisual work.

Practice Tip: copyright.gov is a great source of information on a variety of copyright topics, particularly Circular 1, which covers copyright basics. Other circulars drill down into various topics.

Who May Obtain a Copyright?

Under Section 201(a), for works created after January 1, 1978, a copyright "vests initially in the author or authors of a work," or someone who has succeeded or obtained those rights. The U.S. Supreme Court has stated that the author is "the person who translates the idea into a fixed, tangible expression entitled to copyright protection."

Notice that the above quote referred to a person, but increasingly in music, programs such as Logic Pro and GarageBand create music on their own, or with the aid of whoever is using the program. Who would own the copyright then? Certainly, the person using the program is helping to craft the sounds, but is not actually creating them. Indeed, whole songs and albums can be made in part with the assistance of a computer. Those questions will be dealt with soon. My guess is that the person using the program would actually own the copyright and obtain a license to use the program's sounds when they purchase it.

If many authors contribute to a collective work, their independent contribution is distinctive from the copyright of the collective work. Whoever assembles those independent works into a collective whole is the author of the collective work. Usually, the individual authors will assign their claim to the collective work to the assembler, while potentially maintaining their copyright to the individual piece.

Below are general steps and questions to answer if you own all the rights and are copyrighting a song or an album. Please consult the specific instructions for the form you are filling out. This is taken from Form SR.

* Has the work been published or not/if so, date published?
* Who is the author?
* Are you the only author and owner of the work (or the agent of the individual author who is also the only owner)? Check "NO" to this question if the work was created by multiple individuals (such as, multiple performers, artists, writers) or if any part of this work was prepared as a "work made for hire" for another entity.
* What did author create—music/sound recording/production/lyrics/performance?
* Who is the copyright claimant?

Please identify all known copyright claimant(s) in this work. The author is the original claimant and may always be listed as a claimant, even after the author has transferred rights in the work. The claimant may also be a person or organization to whom copyright has been legally transferred. To be named as a claimant by means of a transfer, a person or organization must own all rights under the U.S. copyright law; ownership of only some of the rights is not sufficient. In addition, a claimant must own the copyright in all the authorship covered by this regulation.

Doing Business As

If the claimant is doing business under another name and as long as the two names represent one and the same entity (such as an unincorporated organization), give this information in a "Note to Copyright Office" on the Certification screen. The relationship may also be expressed as "trading as," "sole owner of," "also known as," and "acceptable alternative designation." Note: Do not refer to a relationship between an individual and a corporation or partnership; such organizations are separate legal entities from individuals associated with them. Thus, "John Smith doing business as XYZ Corporation" is not an acceptable entry.

Transfer of All Rights

A person or organization that is not an author may be named as claimant only if the copyright ownership of all rights was acquired in writing or by operation of law. Written transfers must be signed by the party transferring the copyright or his authorized agent. In addition, copyright ownership may be transferred by the provisions of a will or by operation of law other than by inheritance, for example, by operations of state community property law.

Owner(s) of All Authorship

Do not name as "claimant" someone who owns the copyright in only part of the authorship being claimed. Copyright claimants may not combine their separate claims on a single application form.

Here are tips on using copyright.gov to register your songs or sound recordings. Firstly, it is cheaper and faster to register your works electronically rather than via a paper copy. Typical processing time is 4-6 weeks.

1. Create an account with a username and password just like you would with any other online account.
2. Fill out the proper form depending on what you are copywriting and follow the instructions.
3. If you meet the criteria, register your songs as a collective work. While not common, if you have recorded a bunch of songs and never released them publicly, you could copyright all the unpublished songs as a collective work.
4. Keep in mind the distinction between the author and the claimant/owner.
5. If you are uploading a bunch of songs, do so only a few at a time.
6. You only need to submit the songs to copyright the song. You only need to submit the final sound recording, to copyright that. YOU DO NOT NEED TO SUBMIT LYRICS OR SHEET MUSIC.

Chapter 7

●　　●　　●

MUSIC PUBLISHERS AND TRANSFERS OF COPYRIGHT

Any or all of the copyright owner's exclusive rights listed below, or any subdivision of those rights may be transferred, but the transfer of exclusive rights is not valid unless that transfer is in writing and signed by the owner of the rights conveyed or such owner's duly authorized agent. Transfer of a right on a non-exclusive basis does not require a written agreement. A copyright may also be conveyed by operation of law and may be bequeathed by will or pass as personal property by the applicable laws of intestate succession.

Copyright is a personal property right, and it is subject to the various state laws and regulations that govern the ownership, inheritance, or transfer of personal property as well as terms of contracts or conduct of business. Transfers of copyright are normally made by contract. The Copyright Office does not have any forms for such transfers. The law does provide for the recordation in the Copyright Office of transfers of copyright ownership. Although recordation is not required to make a valid transfer between the parties, it does provide certain legal advantages and may be required to validate the transfer as against third parties.

Music Publishers

If you write songs, you need to know about music publishing. Keep in mind this vital fact: Music publishing only concerns the song copyright, not the sound recording copyright. The term 'music publisher' came about because of the importance of sheet music in the early days of the music business. A songwriter or composer is the creator of a work, which is a song, score or other musical composition. A publisher, on the other hand, is an individual or company that owns or administers the copyright of a work. The writer or creator of the work must assign the copyright to a publisher for that publisher to claim ownership.

The artist handles the creativity and touring, while the publisher takes care of the business end of music. What "business" does the publisher conduct? A publisher finds users (proactive), issues licenses to others who want to use the songwriter's work, collects money, and pays the writer, among other things. In other words, they administer the composition, so these are often call "administrative rights." Most of these last duties are more reactive.

Publishers were powerful in the Tin Pan Alley and Brill Building days when singers did not write their own songs. The publisher decided who had the right of first use and pitched songs of the writers. In those days, the publisher usually received half of the revenue, typically referred to as the "publisher's share." Most songwriters own their own publishing, and may hire someone to do the administrative work for, say, a 10-15% cut. Now, there's also "creative" publishers, who help team songwriters together and assist in that process more.

Types of Publishing Deals

There are generally three types of publishing deals, though there are certainly variations and combinations of all three around. An exclusive deal, usually done in the Tin Pan and Brill eras noted above, is one where the publisher owns the copyright and it is usually 50/50, though if the composer has leverage can be as advantageous as 80/20 in favor of the composer. Please note that in these deals, the split occurs on the NET, not the GROSS, so the publisher's expenses are paid first. This can make a huge difference in any deal. A sub-publishing deal is where the composer owns the copyright, but where the publisher does more than just administer the work; they market the catalog as well. The percentages are usually more advantageous to the songwriter in these deals. Lastly, there is just a straight-up administrative (admin) deal where the publisher is the composer and they just give an entity 10-20% to manage the catalog.

Practice Tip: If you write your own songs, you are your own music publisher unless you find a third party to do so.

As we will see throughout this book, the publisher gets paid for all uses and the sound recording rights holder gets shut out of some payments.

Because of the above, the three major labels all have their own music publishing arms:

1. Universal Music Group (Publishing arm: Universal Music Publishing);
2. Sony Music Entertainment (Publishing arm: Sony/ATV);
3. Warner Music Group (Publishing arm: Warner/Chappell).

So, artists on major labels may be contractually obligated to assign a portion of their publishing to their label. Plus, this allows them new revenue streams given that record labels have lost nearly 75 percent of their revenue from 1999 to 2014. We will discuss all these revenue streams in this book, but any revenue that a song generates is subject to music publishing.

"At a time when record sales and revenues had plummeted, publishing looked like the best bet in the music business, since those companies profited from every soundtrack placement, cover, and commercial use of a song."
---*Martin Bandier, CEO of Sony/ATV Publishing*

As the below diagram illustrates, and we will see this play out further on in this book, many of the laws tend to benefit the composer over the sound recording copyright owner. This is why the labels have started publishing.

If you look at the liner notes on any album from a major label, you will likely see a publishing company listed. Further, if a different songwriter or group of songwriters composes a song, you will likely see a different publishing company for each group.

Practice tip: Liner notes or notes on records and their covers contain vital copyright information.

Now, if you are one of the tens of thousands of songwriters putting out your own music and writing your own songs, then you are, by default, your own publishing company, whether you formally start your own company or not. Please note that from here on out in this book, the term songwriter or publisher can be interchanged when discussing royalties because the publisher is the one who holds the copyright legally. Royalties are the broad term describing money generated by a song. You may also see it referred to as "publishing," though royalties are a broader term.

Songwriters can also transfer their copyrights to companies or even investment funds. The writer would give up all future revenue from their songs in exchange for a lump sum payment. Obviously, the investor is betting the future revenue will be far greater than the payout. There is also a website where songwriters can auction off their songs. Royalty Exchange is a website that allows songwriters, producers, and publishers (anyone with a stake in a song to sell) to put up their piece of the song for sale at auction. The site is not limited to music, but rather all intellectual property. Right now, you must be an accredited investor to invest, and it is possible to buy a portfolio of many different songs, thus diversifying your risk. According to an article in USAToday on June 9, 2014, Royalty Exchange has sold more than $2 million in royalties on more than 2,000 songs, with revenue doubling each month of 2014.

Practice Tip: Unless you have a large discography, most independent songwriters are better off having a third party, such as CD Baby or Tunecore, handle their publishing to make sure they are getting all the money to which they are entitled. I will flesh this out throughout the book.

Getting a third party publisher is vital if your music is being sold, streamed or performed globally because distribution alone does not collect all the money a songwriter is earning. Without adding a publishing collection strategy to the puzzle, a songwriter is probably leaving money on the table.

Traditional Publisher v. a Song Plugger?

In the pre-Dylan and Beatles era, publishers would plug songs to artists, who, by and large, did not write their own material. So, Frank Sinatra, Elvis, and the Drifters would get their material from publishers. These traditional publishers had more power and had the leverage to routinely get half of a song's revenue. Songwriters were happy (and had no choice) to give up half the revenue because otherwise, they would get nothing. Things have changed from this model because most artists and bands write the own material.

When I was starting out writing songs, I would send unsolicited demos to publishers hoping to get a "publishing deal." If such deals still exist, they are rare, and, odds are, they will find you, not the other way around. Or you could ply your trade in Nashville, where some country artists still depend on outside writers, in the hopes of getting someone to record your song. That is a long shot as well. I think a better alternative is to just record and publicize your own music and hope someone covers it so you can get the mechanical royalties (discussed in the next section).

Be wary of paying for plays or paying to get your song placed or pitched. There are many charlatans and scam artists out there who like to prey on songwriters' dreams of discovery. I ran into one years ago. I sent some of my songs out to publishers and one responded with a nice letter. He complimented me on the song, and especially my demo singer. I showed it to her just thinking it was a nice compliment. Unfortunately, she pursued it further and contacted him. He wanted a large sum of money to record demos of other people's songs and shop her around for a record deal, which she always had wanted. She asked me to go in on it, but when I looked into this person's history, I discovered an almost identical letter mailed to another hopeful singer/songwriter. Here was a huge red flag that this person was just fishing for folks with stars in their eyes. My singer friend spent a large amount of money and nothing ever happened.

Sheet Music

I want to touch on sheet music, though not spend a lot of time on it because its importance in the music industry has waned over the years, particularly in this digital age. The publisher or songwriter receives royalties when sheet music of their work is reproduced. Again, it is a copyrighted work. For a single song, the standard royalty is 20% of the marked retail price. For a folio, a collection of songs, it is 10-12.5% of the retail price. For a personality folio, one with the picture of the artist or songs from a particular album (with album's image), add another 5% to the retail price. If a folio contains many different songwriters, then the royalties are pro-rated. For downloadable sheet music, a publisher can get up to half of the revenue, which is higher than physical sheet music. For folios of arrangements of choral or band, the rate is 10% of retail, and if it is only reprinting lyrics, then the rate is 5-7.5% of retail.

Transfers of Copyright

A "transfer of copyright ownership" is defined as "an assignment, mortgage, exclusive license, or any other conveyance, alienation, or hypothecation of a copyright or of any of the exclusive rights comprised in a copyright, whether or not it is limited in time or place of effect, but not including a nonexclusive license." Section 201(d)(2) of the Copyright Act is said to constitute an "explicit statutory recognition of the principle of divisibility of copyright." It provides: "Any of the exclusive rights comprised in a copyright, including any subdivision of any of the rights specified in section 106, may be transferred . . . and owned separately. The owner of any particular exclusive right is entitled, to the extent of that right, to all of the protection and remedies accorded to the copyright owner by this title." Thus, indivisibility is abolished as regards exclusive licensees, who are regarded as the copyright owners of the rights that they have been licensed. "'Copyright owner', with respect to any one of the exclusive rights comprised in a copyright, refers to the owner of that particular right."

But divisibility is provided for only with respect to "[a]ny of the exclusive rights comprised in a copyright, including any subdivision of the rights specified in section 106." Thus, a songwriter could license only a part of the reproduction right by giving someone the exclusive right to reproduce only vinyl records. This grant does convey a copyright, but is only limited to the license.

Transfers in Writing

The statute sets forth separate requirements regarding the instrument of conveyance: it must be "(1) in writing and (2) signed by (3) the owner of the rights conveyed." The requirement of a written instrument, though, applies solely to a "transfer of copyright ownership," which by definition does not include non-exclusive licenses. By negative implication, non-exclusive licenses may therefore be granted orally, or may even be implied from conduct.

Pass Via Will

Section 201(d)(1) of the current Act expressly provides that ownership of copyright "may be bequeathed by will or pass as personal property by the applicable laws of intestate succession." Please note that while Section 204(a) specifies the form for a "transfer" of copyright ownership nothing in the current Act specifies the manner of effectuating a disposition by will. Even if a will is regarded as a "transfer," and this is arguable but not entirely clear from the reference to "any other conveyance, alienation" in the Section 101 definition of "transfer," it seems unlikely that no additional formalities are required to effectuate a transfer by will. It would seem, rather, that the state statute of wills, or comparable legislation would control the mode and manner in which such wills are to be executed and effectuated. In this respect wills appear to differ from other forms of transfer of copyright, even though the state courts have jurisdiction for the enforcement of all such forms of transfer.

Recording a Transfer

Any document "pertaining to a copyright" may be recorded in the Copyright Office provided such document bears the actual signature of the person who executed it, or is accompanied by a sworn or official certification that it is a true copy of the original, signed document. Thus, any assignment, exclusive or nonexclusive license, or any other document pertaining to copyright is susceptible of recordation. Upon receipt of such a document, together with the prescribed fee, the Register of Copyrights is required to record the document, and return it with a certificate of recordation. For a small fee, any interested party can thereupon search for the subject recordation.

The sale or other transfer of ownership of a material object embodying a copyrighted work cannot in and of itself constitute a transfer of the ownership in such copyright. Section 202 states:

Ownership of a copyright, or of any of the exclusive rights under a copyright, is distinct from ownership of any material object in which the work is embodied. Transfer of ownership of any material object, including the copy or phonorecord in which the work is first fixed, does not of itself convey any rights in the copyrighted work embodied in the object; nor, in the absence of an agreement, does transfer of ownership of a copyright or of any exclusive rights under a copyright convey property rights in any material object.

Practice Tip: Copyrights are personal property and, as such, can be transferred and passed on to your heirs. Therefore, state laws regarding that will apply even in this Federal area.

SECTION TWO

● ● ●

THE EXCLUSIVE RIGHTS YOU GET WITH A COPYRIGHT

Chapter 8

• • •

AN OVERVIEW OF THE EXCLUSIVE RIGHTS

Now that we have a foundation of what a copyright is and some key principles, let us dive into the rights you get with your music, along with the revenue streams that emanate from these rights. In general, think of these exclusive rights as protecting a creative work and benefiting the creator. Conversely, if you want to use another's copyrighted work, you generally need permission (a license), unless it involves a compulsory license.

As a general rule, keep in mind that many of the copyright laws benefit the songwriter (the composition copyright) more than the performer or sound recording copyright owner. Thus, you can make more money as the songwriter than the performer, especially with most record deals. If you are both the songwriter and the performer, it's important to imagine yourself split in two. If you are in a rock group, the songwriter(s) can potentially make more money than the other members, and this can create dissention within a group. That is why some groups like U2 and Van Halen credit their songs to the whole group so they can all share in the publishing, though they may divide it however they agree.

A creator or artist receives six exclusive legal rights with a copyright under the Copyright Act.[2] These rights are cumulative and may overlap.[3]

---

2 See 17 U.S.C. 106.

3 House Report at 61.

These six rights are exclusive to the copyright holder, but there are compulsory licenses which are an exception to those exclusive rights: Three of the compulsory licenses are unrelated to music: Cable TV retransmission, jukeboxes, and PBS. But two are big to music: Digital audio transmission of records via digital radio or webcasting (radio shows), and mechanical licenses (mechanicals).

You can assign any of the exclusive copyright protections, and most artists will assign some of those over their careers. These transfers must be in writing. Section 107 through 122 of the Copyright Act imposes limits on the exclusive rights.

We will go through these rights roughly following the path of writing a song, not as Congress adopted these rights, but here is the full text of Section 106:

> Subject to sections 107 through 122 [17 USCS §§ 107 through 122], the owner of copyright under this title has the exclusive rights to do and to authorize any of the following:
>
> (1) to reproduce the copyrighted work in copies or phonorecords;
>
> (2) to prepare derivative works based upon the copyrighted work;
>
> (3) to distribute copies or phonorecords of the copyrighted work to the public by sale or other transfer of ownership, or by rental, lease, or lending;
>
> (4) in the case of literary, musical, dramatic, and choreographic works, pantomimes, and motion pictures and other audiovisual works to perform the copyrighted work publicly;
>
> (5) in the case of literary, musical, dramatic, and choreographic works, pantomimes, and pictorial, graphic, or sculptural works, including the individual images of a motion picture or other audiovisual work, to display the copyrighted work publicly; and
>
> (6) in the case of sound recordings, to perform the copyrighted work publicly by means of a digital audio transmission.

The exclusive rights of the owner of copyright in a sound recording are limited to the rights specified by clauses (1), (2), (3) and (6) of section 106, and do not include any right of performance under section 106(4).

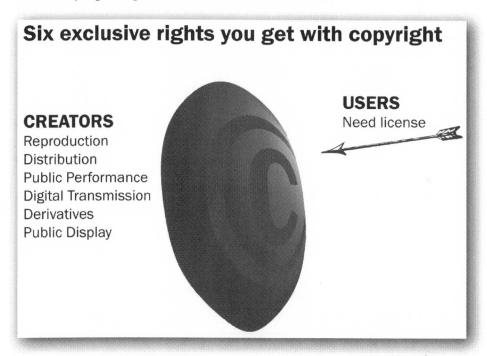

Six exclusive rights you get with copyright

CREATORS
Reproduction
Distribution
Public Performance
Digital Transmission
Derivatives
Public Display

USERS
Need license

Chapter 9

● ● ●

THE RIGHT OF REPRODUCTION 17 U.S.C. 106(1) APPLIES TO BOTH COPYRIGHTS

Introduction

You write a song. That tune in your head you finally put down in a tangible form. Now you want to share it, so a songwriter gets the exclusive right to "reproduce the copyrighted work in copies or phonorecords." No one else can record or copy your song without your permission (you get right of first use). Now, a songwriter can certainly waive this right and allow someone else to record a song they have written before the songwriter records it. In the days before singer/songwriters or even in modern country music in Nashville, most songwriters wrote, or are writing, for other artists.

Mechanical Royalties

The term "mechanicals" emanates from when music was reproduced mechanically on phonograph record or piano roll. There are two main sources of income that songs derive: a mechanical royalty (referred to as "mechanicals") and public performance. We will discuss public performance later, but it is vital you know about mechanicals.

Each time a record label physically reproduces a song, the songwriter earns a Mechanical Royalty, which is a Compulsory License because if a song meets the provisions of Section 115, the publisher is compelled to issue a license.

Such license is usually issued by agency like Harry Fox. So, Harry Fox collects mechanical royalties, passes them on to the publisher, and issues compulsory licenses. This means the songwriter can earn more than the performer, depending on their record deal.

Here are a couple of important points to remember. First, the mechanical is reproduction, not units sold. This means that if a label manufactures a million CDs (not probably done much anymore), in theory they would owe a mechanical on every one. The mechanical applies to downloads, though obviously, nothing is physically reproduced there, so a sale would trigger it. Second, if you put out your own CD or download, there is really no mechanical because you would just be paying yourself. This only applies when you are on a record label or you cover someone else's tune.[4]

Note that you do not need a songwriter's (or publisher's) permission to record a song (cover) once the song has been released and it meets certain other conditions that I will discuss below. If the song has been commercially released, the songwriter/publisher would be entitled to the mechanical. Above we discussed that the songwriter can waive the right of first use. If the song has not been released, the songwriter can deny use, waive the mechanical, or negotiate the mechanical for first use that is different than the rate set by the government. The mechanical royalty rate defines the maximum amount that must be paid to the songwriter for each reproduction once the provisions of Section 115 are met.

For example, Columbia Records hires, or has under contract, Jeff Buckley, who sings, or covers Leonard Cohen's song "Hallelujah". The recording of the song is controlled by Columbia Records (Label), while the song itself is controlled by Leonard Cohen (Songwriter—or, more likely, his publishing company). In Cohen's case, his publishing company is Sony/ATV, which is a subsidiary of his record label. Under U.S. law (and the laws of many nations), each time Cohen's song is physically reproduced, he must be paid the mechanical royalty rate as set by the U.S. government's Copyright Rate Board by the party who reproduces it.

---

4 This is getting in the weeds a bit, but if you are on a major label, the label usually makes you take a smaller mechanical in what is called a "Controlled composition clause."

The mechanical royalty rate in the U.S. is currently 9.1 cents (just under a dime) for each reproduction. It is set by the Copyright Rate Board (CRB).[5] The rate is more for songs longer than five minutes, so cover a short song! And, you pay the mechanical on phonorecords made and distributed as opposed to made and sold. For songs longer than five minutes, the mechanical is 1.75 cents per minute or a fraction thereof, per reproduction. The ringtone rate is 24 cents.[6] The songwriter can waive the mechanical rates or can agree to a lower mechanical rate, which almost always happens when you are on a record label. So, if the songwriter (Cohen) has commercially released his song, anyone who wishes to may cover his song on their release as long as the songwriter is paid the mechanical for each reproduction. In other words, once you release a song, you cannot stop anyone from covering it. However, anyone that covers your song MUST pay you the mechanical royalty rate. If they do not, they have violated the law and you can sue them.

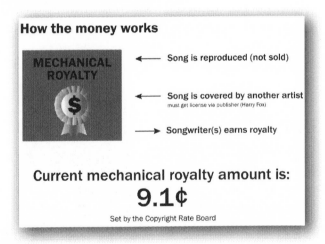

How the money works

Song is reproduced (not sold)

Song is covered by another artist
must get license via publisher (Harry Fox)

Songwriter(s) earns royalty

Current mechanical royalty amount is:

9.1¢

Set by the Copyright Rate Board

---

5 The Copyright Royalty Board is part of the U.S. Library of Congress and it consists of three Copyright Royalty Board judges who determine royalty rates.

6 37 CFR 385(a) - Mechanical Royalty Rates

§ 385.3 Royalty rates for making and distributing phonorecords.

(a) Physical phonorecord deliveries and permanent digital downloads. For every physical phonorecord and permanent digital download made and distributed, the royalty rate payable for each work embodied in such phonorecord shall be either 9.1 cents or 1.75 cents per minute of playing time or fraction thereof, whichever amount is larger.

(b) Ringtones. For every ringtone made and distributed, the royalty rate payable for each work embodied therein shall be 24 cents.

Harry Fox Agency

The compulsory mechanical license is issued mainly through an organization called the Harry Fox Agency. For much more on mechanicals, visit harryfox.com. Thus, the Harry Fox Agency issues licenses to publishers, and the publisher then issues a license to the record company, if any. The Harry Fox Agency is a subsidiary of the National Music Publishers Association. They collect royalties for music publishers when a song is reproduced or copied. If you want to cover a song, you must either get the license through Harry Fox (or one of their competitors) or the publisher directly. Keep in mind, parties can always negotiate a rate other than the statutory rate, specifically if the conditions of section 115 are not met.

Harry Fox (HFA) is the biggest entity that handles licenses for cover songs, but not the only one. Loudr and Easy Song Licensing also handle this, and they will find publishers that are not represented by HFA. There are likely other companies, so search around. They charge a fee for their service, in addition to the mechanicals you must pay to cover the song.

The Compulsory License and Covering Songs

Under Section 115[7] of the Copyright Act, once a song has been recorded and released to the public, anyone else can record it (cover the song) and the copyright holder must license it:

a) To anyone who wants to use it in a phonorecord; audio only recordings, including digital files (downloads),[8] and

b) For a specific payment established by law (the mechanical royalty), and if all the following are met:
1) Song is a non-dramatic musical work; (so not used originally in a musical or opera);
2) Song previously recorded;

---

7 While I do not reprint the whole section due to space limitations, I urge you to read the entire section.
8 Added in 1995.

3) Distributed publicly in phonorecords; audio-only recordings, so this does not apply to DVDs, so movies must negotiate with every publisher for home video use and the publisher can charge whatever they want for it; phonorecords also mean downloads;

4) New recording does not change the basic melody or fundamental character of song ("to conform it to the style or manner of interpretation of the performance")[9], and;

5) New recording is used only in phonorecords.

All five conditions must be met or else the songwriter/publisher does not have to issue license or can negotiate a different (higher) mechanical rate, although nearly all songs meet the above criteria. The reason for this compulsory license, a huge exception to the exclusive right of reproduction was that Congress thought copyright holders were getting too much power and were becoming a monopoly.

You must get the license, even if you are giving away the song for free because mechanicals are paid on reproductions, not records sold. It does not matter if the cover makes money. Note that the compulsory license does not apply to sound recordings. You cannot just duplicate a prior sound recording and claim it is a compulsory license under Section 115.

A compulsory licensee is required to pay the copyright owner a royalty for every phonorecord (containing the copyright owner's licensed musical work) "made and distributed in accordance with the license." Thus, if a single phonorecord contains more than one copyrighted musical work, a separate royalty payment is due for each work contained on the same phonorecord. This means that every time a composer's song is reproduced, the writer gets a mechanical royalty. The term's origin is when music was mechanically reproduced.

Under Section 115, a mechanical royalty is not payable unless the phonorecord is both "made" and "distributed." For these purposes, the term "made" is intended to be broader than "manufactured," and includes every possible manufacturing or other process capable of reproducing a sound recording in phonorecords. A phonorecord is considered "distributed" for this purpose

9 Section 115(a)(2) of Copyright Act.

only if the person exercising the compulsory license has voluntarily and permanently parted with its possession. Given that there are no physical products in downloads, a sale triggers the royalty obligation.

In general, the artist doing the cover (licensee) owns the resulting sound recording. The licensee generally pays the mechanical. A performer triggers the compulsory license by filing a notice of intention to obtain a compulsory license, or by just obtaining the license itself from the publisher. That person thereby obtains the right to make and distribute phonorecords. With that right, he also incurs the royalty obligation. Therefore, the individual whose name appears in the notice of intention is liable for all royalties payable under the compulsory license obtained pursuant to that notice.

Failure to file reports and make the payments will result in the license being terminated, and all phonorecords made without paying the mechanical will be considered acts of infringement. The compulsory license confers on the licensee a non-exclusive reproduction right in a given non-dramatic musical work. The activity that triggers a Section 115 compulsory license is the distribution "to the public in the United States under the authority of the copyright owner" of phonorecords of the non-dramatic musical work subject to the license. It should be noted that the compulsory license does not grant you the right to reprint the lyrics. In theory, you would have to go to the publisher and negotiate this, though if you pay the mechanical, most will likely let you reprint lyrics in liner notes.

You must get the license before, or within 30 days after recording the cover, and prior to distributing it. If you cannot find the songwriter of the tune you want to cover, you must file notice of the compulsory license with the Copyright Office. Under 17 U.S.C. 115(b):

(1)   Any person who wishes to obtain a compulsory license under this section shall, before or within thirty days after making, and before distributing any phonorecords of the work, serve notice of intention to do so on the copyright owner. If the registration or other public records of the Copyright Office do not identify the copyright owner and include an address at which notice can be served, it shall be sufficient to file the notice of intention in the Copyright Office.

The notice shall comply, in form, content, and manner of service, with requirements that the Register of Copyrights shall prescribe by regulation.

(2) Failure to serve or file the notice required by clause (1) forecloses the possibility of a compulsory license and, in the absence of a negotiated license, renders the making and distribution of phonorecords actionable as acts of infringement under section 501 and fully subject to the remedies provided by sections 502 through 506 and 509.

Much of Section 115 has to do with payments, royalty rates and regulatory language. There needs to be monthly statements and payments to copyright holders for the mechanicals, and if there's not, "the owner may give written notice to the licensee that, unless the default is remedied within thirty days from the date of the notice, the compulsory license will be automatically terminated." Such termination renders either the making or the distribution, or both, of all phonorecords for which the royalty has not been paid, actionable as acts of infringement under section 501 and fully subject to the remedies provided by sections 502 through 506." The statute appears to be absolute: that failure to serve or file the notice in the required manner "forecloses the possibility of a compulsory license."[10]

Practice Tip: Covers are a great way for a band to get noticed, but it is important to get the compulsory license, pay the mechanicals, and comply with Section 115 or risk legal problems.

Four ways to find the publisher/songwriter:

1. Copyright search at copyright.gov
2. harfyfox.com or similar company
3. BMI or ASCAP search
4. Google or online search

---

10 17 U.S.C. § 115(b)(2).

Remember when I listed four good reasons to register your songs with the Copyright Office? One of those reasons was collecting mechanical royalties, and you cannot collect them without registering them.[11]

How Much Can You Change Your Cover?

Most of the criteria that must be met before you can cover someone else's song (or they can cover yours) is straight forward, but I did want to touch on what exactly it means to NOT change the basic melody or fundamental character of a song. Obviously, there's not a bright line here and many covers use a different arrangement or take some liberties with the song they are covering— otherwise, why even do a cover?

17 U.S.C. 115(a)(2) states:

A compulsory license includes the privilege of making a musical arrangement of the work to the extent necessary to conform it to the style or manner of interpretation of the performance involved, but the arrangement shall not change the basic melody or fundamental character of the work, and shall not be subject to protection as a derivative work under this title, except with the express consent of the copyright owner.

Translation: Do not change the basic melody (really not a cover then). But, the arrangement is fine to change. Indeed, why cover a song if you are going to do the same arrangement? Cover versions often have vastly different arrangements to their original. Paul Anka did swing versions of rock songs such as Nirvana's "Smells Like Teen Spirit". Your cover, however, is not protected as a derivative work.

If you cover a song, or someone covers your song, the words cannot be changed to any great extent and the song must be in the same language as the original. So, if someone wants to do a Spanish version of your English song, they will need to get permission from you. As the songwriter, you can

---

11 The law states:

To be entitled to receive royalties under a compulsory license, the copyright owner must be identified in the registration or other public records of the Copyright Office. The owner is entitled to royalties for phonorecords made and distributed after being so identified, but is not entitled to recover for any phonorecords previously made and distributed. 17 U.S.C. 115(c)(1).

certainly change the lyrics or do whatever you want to your own songs (make a derivative work). I get asked about what "Weird Al" does a lot, and he clearly transforms the songs he covers because he changes the lyrics. He could argue that it is parody (a fair use defense we will discuss later), but he always gets permission from the publisher and has never been sued.

In the original Copyright Act, your arrangement could not allow the original song to be "perverted, distorted or travestied."[12] I doubt this standard would apply today. In fact, I do not even know what that would entail to "pervert" the original. If the cover is that different from the original, then the license would not apply since it would be a different song using the lyrics of the original. Certainly, some covers add greatly to the original, and sometimes are more popular, for example, Jeff Buckley's (and many others') cover of Leonard Cohen's "Hallelujah". While the person doing the cover may own some or all the sound recording (unlikely if on a major label though), they will not even own what contributions they make in addition to the cover that are original without the publisher's permission. This can be an issue in jazz where straight-up covers are rare, and the musicians often improvise based on the cover, but take it into original territory.

The problem is that obtaining a compulsory license does not protect the original musical contributions added in the subsequent artist's rendition. That is, compulsory licensees convey only the right to record and distribute the underlying work. A separate copyright does not automatically attach to otherwise copyrightable derivative material. Thus, if a musician wishes to protect his additions, he must still seek permission from the underlying copyright holder in order to receive a derivative work copyright. Jazz musicians, however, almost never seek permission from the copyright holder to create a derivative work, and instead rely on the compulsory licensing scheme.[13]

---

12 H.R. Rep. No. 2222, 60th Cong., 2d Sess. 6 at 109 (1909).

13 This scheme leaves those otherwise copyrightable aspects of the jazz musician's arrangement and solo improvisation vulnerable to unauthorized transcriptions and use. For example, it is widespread practice in the sheet music industry to sell books containing transcribed jazz solos—sales from which the jazz artist receives no royalties. While a sheet music company would be required to pay the music publishers and owners of the composition copyright for use of Art Tatum's transcribed arrangement and solo of "Cherokee" by Ray Noble, it would not be required to pay Art Tatum—even for a book entitled The Art Tatum Solo Book.

Conclusion on Reproduction

The songwriter gets paid the mechanical royalty, usually collected by an agent from the person who covers it via Harry Fox Agency. The sound recording holder gets nothing. This can be a big source of revenue for a songwriter.

Bill Monroe on Elvis' version of "Blue Moon of Kentucky": "Them were powerful checks."

Don McLean on what "American Pie" means: "It means I'll never have to work again."

While reproduction and distribution are often intertwined, they are different. A record company hires a plant to make CDs/vinyl (reproduce it), but not distribute it. This leads us to the second exclusive right. You do not need a mechanical license if you are recording and distributing a song you wrote yourself because you would be paying yourself. You also do not need a license if the song is in the public domain. If you are not sure if the song you are looking to license is in the public domain, and therefore does not require license authority, we suggest you use the search on www.pdinfo.com.

Note, Jazz Has Got Copyright Law and That Ain't Good, 118 Harv. L. Rev. 1940, 1945–1946 (2005).

Chapter 10

● ● ●

THE RIGHT OF DISTRIBUTION 17 U.S.C. 106(3)
APPLIES TO BOTH COPYRIGHTS

Introduction

Returning to our song, it has been written and recorded. We have made copies under the first right, and now the author/owner gets the exclusive right to distribute the song and sound recording. It does not make much sense to make copies of something if you are not going to distribute them. Thus, the songwriter has the right "to distribute copies or phonorecords of the copyrighted work to the public by sale or other transfer of ownership, or by rental, lease, or lending." With respect to CDs, vinyl, or downloads ("phonorecords"), this simply means no one can sell, rent, or lease copies of your songs without an agreement in place. So, if you are an artist who releases your own records, and you want someone to distribute copies of your records (either physically or digitally), you must enter an agreement with the distributor to do so. The copyright owner therefore possesses the exclusive right to sell, give away, rent, or lend any material embodiment of his work.[14]

In the two worlds of music I have discussed, here's your distribution breakdown. If you are on any record label, you very likely give them the right to reproduce and distribute your music. Indeed, those are two reasons you are

---

14 Ortiz-Gonzalez v. Fonovisa, 277 F.3d 59, 62 (1st Cir. 2002). See Cable/Home Communication Corp. v. Network Prods., Inc., 902 F.2d 829, 843 (11th Cir. 1990).

on a major label, and both of those functions are in the definition of record labels that I discussed in Section One. Conversely, if you are a band or artist on your own, you are your own record label.

Not only are there the two worlds of music, there are two types of music distribution: physical and digital music. For physical music, you can distribute your music yourself at shows, sell it on your website, give it away, try to get a record store to stock it, or try to get independent distribution (very hard to do). If you are a DIY (do-it-yourself) artist, the only way to get your music distributed digitally on iTunes or Amazon is to use a third party company like CD Baby and TuneCore. They are the two biggest, but there are others, so do your research. CD Baby also does physical music duplication via Disc Makers and will sell physical music for indie artists.

The definition of publication in Section 101 is practically synonymous with the definition of distribution in 17 U.S.C. 106(3). Congress used the terms interchangeably in the legislative history and appear to broaden the definition of publish to include the right to distribute. They also wanted to soften the harshness of failure to publish without proper notice that existed under older versions of the Copyright Act.

The offering to distribute copies or phonorecords to a group of persons for purposes of further distribution, public performance, or public display, constitutes publication. This language signals that Congress intended to trigger "publication" merely by offering works of authorship to the public—i.e., making them available. In fact, the timing, circumstances, and reasons for adding this language to the definition of publication illuminates Congress' intent on that issue both with respect to the defined term "publication" and the undefined term "distribution".

But not just any distribution of copies or phonorecords falls within this right. It is limited to such distributions as are made "to the public."[15] There was very little litigation over violating the distribution right when all music was physical. The focus was more on the reproduction violation. But the advent of Napster in 1999 brought the scope of the distribution right to center stage as

---

15 Litecubes, LLC v. N. Light Prods., 523 F.3d 1353, 1371 (Fed. Cir.).

copyright owners began to pursue enterprises operating file-sharing networks and those using these networks.[16]

In Harper & Row, Publishers, Inc. v. Nation Enterprises,[17] the Supreme Court equated the distribution right with the "the exclusive right of publications," by reference to the Act's extensive legislative history.[18] That construction faithfully reflects Congress' extensive efforts to link distribution with publication. The Court added that Section 106(3) "recognize[s] for the first time a distinct statutory right of first publication, which had previously been an element of the common-law protections afforded unpublished works." The opinion went out of its way to confer special solicitude on the right of first publication in safeguarding it against a capacious fair use construction, calling that right "inherently different from other Section 106 rights," insofar as only one person can be the first publisher.[19]

It should be noted that a public performance of a work, even if unauthorized, does not infringe the distribution right. As such, liability for that conduct lies outside the distribution right. On the other hand, distribution of infringing copies to a public group for the purpose of public performance does implicate the distribution right, even if the performance per se is licensed or exempt from liability.[20]

Downloads (e.g. iTunes)

I have not specifically discussed this topic, so now that we have covered reproduction and distribution, this is a good spot to cover downloads. As I stated, downloads are strictly a mechanical at the full statutory rate. Ringtones are 24 cents per download. Downloads used to be very popular, but single-track

---

16 See Hotaling v. Church of Jesus Christ of Latter-Day Saints, 118 F.3d 199, 203 (4th Cir. 1997).

17 471 U.S. 539 (1985).

18 Id. at 552.

19 Id. at 552

20 See Agee v. Paramount Communications, Inc., 59 F.3d 317, 325 (2d Cir. 1995); UMG Recordings, Inc. v. Hummer Winblad Venture Ptnrs. (In reNapster, Inc),377 F. Supp. 2d 796, 804 (N.D. Cal. 2005).

download sales in the US have crashed by 42% since their peak just four years ago, sparking the real possibility that they could become a dead format within five years.

For a digital store to sell music, it must have the song files on its own hard drives/servers. This allows the store to control the customer experience, provide customer support and control the shopping cart and checkout process. When a song is bought or played online, it is the digital store that is fulfilling the download or stream. This is where the problem is. For a digital store to legally fulfill a stream or download, it must get global licenses and make direct payments to copyright holders or the entities that represent them.

As an example, a "download music store" like AmazonMP3 or iTunes sells a song file. This song replicates itself onto your hard drive where it sits for you to access and play whenever you want. It is a one-time sale. The digital store only needs a license to the recording of the song (the sound recording) to sell it.[21] For the digital store to get the right to this copyright, it must negotiate directly with the record label that controls it, or the independent artist. There are no pre-existing laws or rules in place that dictate how much the digital store must pay the label for each sale. This is a one-to-one negotiation with each side jockeying for the best deal terms--the label wants as much money as possible while the store wants to pay out as little as possible. This is what a contract between a record label and iTunes or Amazon is all about. So, independent artists are on their own with regard to this, or can use sites such as Tunecore and CD Baby to distribute their music.

Once this license is in place, and a song is sold via download from the digital store, the digital store pays the record label for sale of the recording. The record label then handles paying and administering any other money owed to copyright holders. This includes money owed to the person(s) that own(s) the song. The laws around the world state that each time a song is "reproduced" (a download is legally considered to be a "reproduction") the person(s) who wrote the song must get paid a mechanical royalty.

---

21 This is not always the case outside of the US.

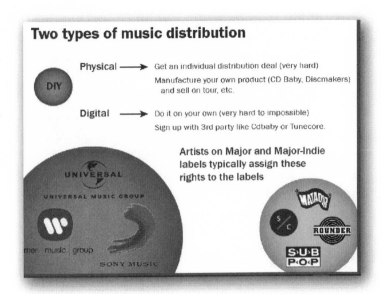

Below are two screenshots from CD Baby. The first one indicates the different packages they offer for physical and digital distribution, and streaming. The second illustrates all the platforms on which an artist can either sell or stream their music.

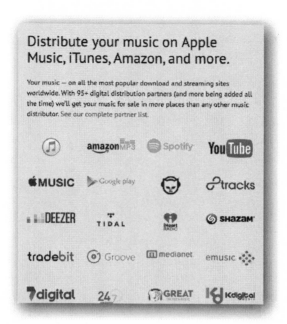

First Sale Doctrine (exception to the exclusive right to distribute)

Once you buy an album, the copyright holder's exclusive right of distribution (and publication) ends because the music has already been distributed. As an example, if I buy a CD, I can give it away, lend it to a friend, or sell it. This concept is known as the "first sale doctrine." This doctrine makes it possible for used record stores to exist and for libraries to lend out music. There are limits to what you can do under this doctrine that I will discuss below.

The First Sale Doctrine has been codified in Section 109(a), and it provides that the distribution right may be exercised solely with respect to the initial disposition of copies of a work, not to prevent or restrict the resale or other further transfer of possession of those copies.[22] Moreover, although the initial distribution of that copy may be a sale, the same result occurs if it is a gift or any other transfer of title in the copy. The more accurate terminology

---

22 Kirtsaeng v. John Wiley & Sons, Inc., ___ U.S. ___, 133 S. Ct. 1351, 1368, 185 L. Ed. 2d 392 (2013); UMG Recordings, Inc. v. Augusto, 558 F. Supp. 2d 1055, 1059 (C.D. Cal. 2008), aff'd, 628 F.3d 1175 (9th Cir. 2011).

would not be "first sale" but rather "first authorized disposition by which title passes."[23]

Regarding this doctrine, here are the questions you should ask:

(a) was the subject physical product (the "copy") lawfully manufactured with authorization of the copyright owner;

(b) was that particular copy transferred under the copyright owner's authority;

(c) does defendant qualify as the lawful owner of that particular copy; and

(d) did defendant thereupon dispose of that particular copy (as opposed to, for example, reproducing it)?

If you answered "yes" to any of the above, you can utilize the First Sale defense.

In the *Augusto* case referred to in the footnotes above, Universal Music distributed CDs to music industry insiders, labeled as "promotional," to advertise the release of new recordings. This is a common practice. They usually had different artwork and tracks than the ultimate commercial release. The legend stamped on the discs stated that the pertinent CD "is the property of the record company and is licensed to the intended recipient for personal use only." Acceptance also purported to create "an agreement to comply with the terms of the license."[24] The defendant received nothing from Universal Music, but managed to obtain numerous such promotional CDs from music shops, which he proceeded to market via eBay as "rare collectibles not available in stores." His efforts brought in not only revenue but also a suit for copyright infringement.

The court adopted the four elements set forth above. It found undisputed the facts that Universal Music lawfully manufactured the subject discs, which Augusto never copied. As to the remaining two questions—did Universal Music transfer ownership of the promotional CDs, making Augusto their lawful owner, Judge Otero determined that they collapsed into the question

---

23 Id.
24 *Augusto* at 1058.

whether Universal Music transferred "title to the music industry insiders when it mailed them the Promo CDs."

The district court opinion resolved that question resoundingly in Augusto's favor. It held that the so-called "license language" on the discs' label failed to make their transfer into a license rather than a sale (in this instance, a gift). In looking to the "economic realities" of the situation, the court noted that Universal Music parted with perpetual possession of the plastic forming those particular promo CDs, such that the industry recipients could keep them forever or even throw them in the trash, if they desired. It kept no records of recipients, so it could not reclaim the CDs even if it wanted to do so.[25]

The Section 109(a) immunity applies only if the copies at issue have been "lawfully made under this title." Therefore, if manufacture of a copy infringes the reproduction or adaptation right, its distribution will infringe the distribution right, even if done by the owner of that copy, and even if the distributor, in acquiring ownership of the copy from an infringing manufacturer, had no notice of plaintiff's copyright. "For example, any resale of an illegally 'pirated' phonorecord would be an infringement ... ."[26]

Leasing Phonorecords

In order to meet this threat to the record industry, Congress adopted the Record Rental Amendment of 1984. That amendment modifies the first sale doctrine incorporated into Section 109(a) in several particulars. Music stores were leasing records to fans, who would then make copies and return the CD in a day or so. Record sales declined and they lobbied Congress to stop this practice, and they did. Non-profit libraries and educational institutions are exempt however. Further, it must be done for non-profit reasons.[27]

---

25 Id. at 1061.

26 Metal Morphosis, Inc. v. Acorn Media Publ'g, Inc., 639 F. Supp. 2d 1367, 1372 (N.D. Ga. 2009).

27 17 U.S.C. § 109(b)(1)(A).

The ReDigi Case

The above section on the First Sale doctrine applies only to physical music. You can see and touch the music, so it is fairly straightforward. But, what about downloaded music via digital files? Again, this will be a constant theme throughout this book. Much of the Copyright Act was written long before the advent of the internet, digital media, and MP3 files. So, courts and those in the music business must apply archaic and outdated law to modern circumstances.

ReDigi is a company who thought that if the First Sale doctrine applied to physical music, it should also apply to digital music. If I am tired of an album, I can always sell or give it away. ReDigi figured the same would be true of digital music and they wanted to give people a chance to sell their "used" digital files they no longer wanted. So, ReDigi would rip those files from a person's device, and put them on their server to re-sell. They got permission from no one, and Capital Records, who owns lots of valuable sound recordings, sued them for violating their reproduction and distribution rights. In Capitol Records, LLC v. ReDigi,,Inc.[28] the court had to address the novel question of whether a digital music file, lawfully made and purchased, may be resold by its owner through ReDigi under the first sale doctrine. For a great summation of this issues, go to Npr.org and search the case.

ReDigi calls itself a "virtual marketplace for pre-owned digital music." The Court said this case is a fundamental clash over culture, policy, and copyright law. In the end, the judge sided with Capitol Records. He wrote:

. . . the fact that a file has moved from one material object — the user's computer — to another — the ReDigi server — means that a reproduction has occurred. Similarly, when a ReDigi user downloads a new purchase from the ReDigi website to her computer, yet another reproduction is created. It is beside the point that the original phonorecord no longer exists. It matters only that a new phonorecord has been created.[29]

Further, the Court found that the First Sale doctrine does not apply if there has already been a reproduction violation:

---

28 934 F.Supp.2d 640 (S.D.N.Y. 2013)

29 ReDigi at 650.

ReDigi is not "lawfully made under this title." 17 U.S.C. § 109(a). Moreover, the statute protects only distribution by "the owner of a particular copy or phonorecord ... of that copy or phonorecord." Id. Here, a ReDigi user owns the phonorecord that was created when she purchased and downloaded a song from iTunes to her hard disk. But to sell that song on ReDigi, she must produce a new phonorecord on the ReDigi server. Because it is therefore impossible for the user to sell her "particular" phonorecord on ReDigi, the first sale statute cannot provide a defense. Put another way, the first sale defense is limited to material items, like records, that the copyright owner put into the stream of commerce. Here, ReDigi is not distributing such material items; rather, it is distributing reproductions of the copyrighted code embedded in new material objects, namely, the ReDigi server in Arizona and its users' hard drives. The first sale defense does not cover this any more than it covered the sale of cassette recordings of vinyl records in a bygone era.[30]

Conclusion

The following diagram illustrates where the law is at with the First Sale Doctrine.

1st Sale Doctrine

What you CAN do	What you CAN'T do
• Sell/give away your physical music	• Make copies of physical music to sell/give away
• Make a copy of your physical music for your own personal use	• Resell a burned CD from one you downloaded
• Download an album and burn it for you personal use	• Re-sell individual digital tracks
• Sell/give away your personal device that contains your music	

---

30 ReDigi at 655.

According to Nimmer, someone "who makes copies or phonorecords of a work infringes the copyright owner's reproduction right under Section 106(1), even if he does not also infringe the Section 106(3) distribution right by sale or other disposition of those copies or phonorecords." [31]While this may be technically true, what would the damages be if I recorded an album on a cassette for my personal use in my car? What about the common example of burning a downloaded album to a CD? Purely personal reproduction is so prolific and is so impossible to enforce, that its violation is de minimis.

---

31 Nimmer 8.02[C]

Chapter 11

● ● ●

THE RIGHT TO PUBLIC PERFORMANCE 17 U.S.C. 106(4) APPLIES ONLY TO SONG COPYRIGHT

You have written your song and recorded it. You get the right to make copies and distribute them, and the songwriter gets the right to "perform the copyrighted work publicly."

If you read the literal language above, you can more than infer that only the songwriter can perform the song publicly. Well, that would be impossible to police and we want music and all art to grow and disseminate, so the songwriter/publisher can collect royalties when their song is played in public either by themselves or someone else.

There are two main sources of income for songwriters as it relates to public performance. We discussed the first in mechanicals, and here is the second source—public performance. Within public performance, there are two sub-categories:

1) the songwriter or others singing a particular song in public, and
2) pre-recorded public performance.

In this section, we will focus on live music. Thus, the right to public performance is a broad one, and it means the songwriter gets to perform the song in clubs, via a DJ, radio, TV, or anywhere in public, and receives money when others perform their tune in the same manner.

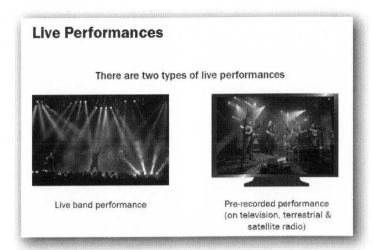

Practice Tip: When talking about live music performance, ONLY THE SONGWRITER/PUBLISHER GETS PAID. The sound recording owner gets shut out from this.

Therefore, this area has generally two sides. If you are a business, you cannot play music publicly without a license. Copyright laws require music users to get permission from songwriters and composers who can charge a fee before their music is played publicly, which then allows them to continue to create music (in theory). That fee is collected by what are called Performing Rights Organizations (PROs), who then, in theory, forward that on to the musicians, minus the PROs administrative expenses.

PROs

The two biggest PROs in the U.S. are BMI (Broadcast Music, Inc.) and ASCAP (American Society of Composers, Authors, and Publishers). Only songwriters can join a PRO, and if you are one, you should join. I am a member of BMI, though I do not think there's much difference between the two; they essentially act as a duopoly.[32] Do your due diligence before joining both and check out their websites for further information: bmi.com or ascap.com.

---

32 They have both been acting under consent decrees by the US Dept. of Justice.

Performing Rights Organizations (PROs)

Copyright holder registers songs with PROs

PROs divide royalties into two "shares"
- 50% Publisher share
- 50% Songwriter share

You cannot belong to more than one PRO at a time, though you can switch. BMI has you agree to a two-year deal initially but is free to join. ASCAP charges you $50 to join. A third PRO, with around 10 percent of the market is SESAC, which started in Europe. SESAC is a for-profit corporation and you must be accepted to join. BMI and ASCAP are not-for-profit and take all composers.

Recall in Section One, when I discussed publishing, and the old throwback of half going to the publisher and the other half going to the composers. Well, that old system is still used by the two big PROs. If you sign up with ASCAP as a songwriter, you also need to register a "vanity publishing company." So, create a name, and register your publishing company with ASCAP. You must do this to get paid all your money (the publisher's share). This all costs money.[33] You also need to register your publishing company as an LLC (limited liability company) and open a bank account in that name so you can cash the ASCAP checks made out to your publishing company. ASCAP pays out 50% of the total money to the songwriter and 50% to the publisher. If you do not register a publishing company, you will only get half of your money.

---

33 There is a $150 fee for solely owned publishing companies to affiliate (just your own music); $250 for partnerships, corporations, and limited-liability companies (these could be either just one writer's song, or a company that owns several writers' songs). There is no fee to affiliate with BMI solely as a writer.

If you are an unaffiliated songwriter with BMI, you don't need to register a vanity publishing company, but make sure you claim a 200% share when you register your song with them—only then will BMI pay you 100% of the money.

Practice Tip: Songwriters need to register their songs with their PRO. That's how they know when their song gets played. Also, if you play live, submit your set list to your PRO. They both have portals to do so.

You must register your songs with a PRO so they know when your song is played publicly. If you have not affiliated with a PRO yet, signup for an admin publishing company first (like CD Baby or Tunecore), and they will then register your songs with a PRO. You can certainly hire a third party to be your publisher even if you have already joined a PRO. We will discuss this more in Section Three.

What the PROs DO NOT Collect for Songwriters—The Publisher's Share v. The Songwriter's Share

As we have discussed, the PROs do not collect mechanicals. Further, the PROs will only collect public performances in the U.S., so those overseas (if there are any) will likely not be collected. ASCAP considers the publisher's share and songwriter's share to each be 50% of total performance royalties. BMI talks about these same splits as 100% for the publisher and 100% for the songwriter. It gets a little confusing, but they're essentially talking about the same money split up in exactly the same way. It's just that ASCAP uses percentages that are based on total performance royalties (thus 50/50), while BMI splits those halves first, and then distributes 100% of each half to the appropriate entities.

Practice Tip: If you write your own songs, you are your own publisher until you get a third party to do so.

The 50/50 split is likely left over from the early Tin Pan Alley days of music when publishers had more power and earned half of a song's royalties. Most performers did not write their own songs, so they relied on publishers to find the material. Thus, they played a vital role in the industry.

The shares system still rears its head though. If you noticed from the Sam Smith and Tom Petty settlement (discussed more fully below), Petty and co-writer Jeff Lynne were each given a 12.5% writing credit. If you understand the publisher's share, this math makes sense. Smith and his two co-writers each split the 50% writer's share of the tune, with the publisher taking half. Now, with two more writers, their share is cut in half, and Petty and Lynne split the 25%, which is 12.5%.

But even if you've set up a publishing company and affiliated with a PRO as both the writer and the publisher, it is just too small a publishing company for the PROs to notice. That's why you should have a third party handle your admin publishing. Most songwriters do not have the clout or means to do all the administrative work that a "real" (i.e. big) publishing company can. And that means that PROs have less incentive when it comes to collecting every cent an indie songwriter is owed—they do not have skin in the game so to speak. Therefore, if a songwriter gets paid only their songwriter's share of performance royalties, the other 50% is likely going to go uncollected.

This seems like a bad deal for indie songwriters, but the simple solution is to join a 3rd party distribution company like CD Baby or Tunecore, and have them collect that for you. In other words, they act, and will likely be, your publisher for the sake of collecting these monies. Plus, a 3rd party publisher can collect all the mechanicals and public performance royalties you are due.

Venues that Play Music

If you have live music, you must get a license from a PRO. There's really no way out of it for the most part. What is a "public performance?" It is anything beyond singing for friends and family in a private setting. Although, if you regularly have house concerts, that would be a public performance. Certainly, there is no bright line. If I performed on a street corner, that is "public," but no one pays a PRO. Yet, if a city has a street festival with music, they would need a license for it.

Club owners pay the PROs a flat annual license fee that allows artists to perform copyrighted music in their club. This is how any artist can stand up on any stage and sing a Bob Dylan song. The PROs use a variety of methods (including visiting clubs) to determine which songs are being publicly performed.

Practice Tip: You do not need a license to play a song in public—the venue does. The mechanical compulsory license is only triggered upon reproduction (not even recording).

Here are some answers to common questions from the PROs' websites.

* From BMI.com: Does a business need to belong to a PRO if we only play "original material"?
  The term "original music" generally means musical works written by the performing musicians. That does not mean, however, that the musicians are not affiliated with a PRO. This is because licensing organizations like BMI are the vehicles through which songwriters and composers are compensated for the public performances of their music. In addition, one of the purposes of BMI is to help foster the development of up-and-coming songwriters, many of whom perform in public areas and establishments. Many times, these performers are asked to play a song known by the general public that was written by someone else to add to the entertainment. This performance also requires permission.

* From ASCAP.com: Who does ASCAP collect from?

Look for the ASCAP Customer sticker! This indicates that an establishment is compensating music creators by paying an ASCAP license fee. Once you've registered your works with ASCAP, they become part of the ASCAP repertory for which we collect performance royalties. We do this by negotiating with and collecting license fees from the users of music—our customers—who perform the works in our repertory.

Factors for charging Bars/Restaurants:

* whether the music is live/recorded;
* whether it is synced with videos;
* seating capacity;
* how many musicians and nights are you playing;
* is admission charged.

For concert venues:

* venue's seating capacity and ticket prices

I have called BMI regarding what they charge a small house concert venue of about 40 seats. I was told a blanket license would be $234/year or eight percent of the gross receipts from the concert ticket (excluding other sales), whichever is greater. On the flip side, an artist who tours and plays venues of 500 or less can earn about $10 a show.

Registering Your Works (taken from BMI.com)

BMI enters work registrations into its databases from one of two sources, (1) a BMI song registration form provided either electronically or on paper, or (2) a cue sheet which details all music written specifically for a film or television show, or other audio-visual work, typically prepared by the production company.

All songs must be submitted to BMI via a BMI registration form in order to receive credit for certain types of performances (e.g., all radio, commercial music services, commercial jingles and promotional announcements, live pop and classical concerts and Internet). A registration received from any songwriter, composer or publisher of a work will suffice to credit all participants. If the publisher submits a registration, the writer does not have to submit one as well, and vice versa. However, we strongly encourage each co-publisher of a work to submit its own song registration form to assure that the work is entered into the publisher's correct BMI account. BMI will enter the work into its database for the shares and participants indicated on the first registration received. If a later registration is received for the same work which conflicts with the earlier registration, we will notify the party submitting the later registration and request documentation or written confirmation from all affected participants in conformity with BMI's conflicting registration rules before changing our records.

For BMI to make payment on time for the public performance of your music, it is imperative that all registrations (both songs and cue sheets) be received as close to the performance date as possible. It is essential that you register all your works in order that BMI can provide information about your entire catalogue to foreign performing rights organizations, and so that BMI may quickly and easily identify foreign royalties received on your behalf.

Samples, Medleys and Parodies

BMI accepts for registration works which "sample" other works, provided all parties have agreed to the share percentages on the new work. These shares cannot exceed 200%. The percentages must be noted on the BMI registration form for the work and a copy of the sample license agreement must be provided to BMI upon request. Standard rates for a popular song will be paid. The same rules apply when two or more works are utilized in a single recording as a medley.

A parody is a satirical imitation of a work. Permission from the owner of the copyright is generally required before commercial exploitation of a parody. BMI will credit the parody based upon the shares authorized by the publisher of the parodied work.

How Royalties Are Divided

BMI considers payments to songwriters or composers and to publishers as a single unit equal to 200%. Where there is the usual division of performance royalties between songwriters or composers and publishers, the total writers' shares will be 100% (half of the available 200%), and the total publishers' shares will be the remaining 100%.

Please note the following rules with respect to the division of the 200% royalty:

The total publishers' shares may not exceed 100%. If the agreement between the publishers and songwriters or composers provides for the songwriters or composers to receive more than 100%, the work should be registered with BMI indicating the percentages allocable to all songwriters or composers and all publishers so that the total is not more than 200%.[34]

Where no performing rights (or only partial performing rights) have been assigned to a publisher, the songwriters or composers will receive the entire 200% (or the balance of the entire 200%) in the same ratio as their respective writer shares. However, a songwriter or composer who has assigned to a publisher all or part of his or her proportionate rights in the publisher's share shall not be entitled to receive any portion of the remainder of the publisher's share allocable to his or her co-writer(s).

---

34 Note that this is subject to change via the DOJ's "100 Percent Licensing" ruling that I discuss later.

Example: John and Mary wrote "Their Song" together. John signed a songwriter agreement with Music Publisher. Mary did not. When the work is registered with BMI, John will list his writer share as 50%, Mary will list her writer share as 100% (50% for her co-writer interest and 50% for her unassigned publisher interest) and Music Publisher will list its publisher share as 50% (for the publisher's interest it obtained from John). If Mary later assigns her publisher interest to the same Music Publisher, Mary will notify BMI, her writer share will be reduced to 50% and Music Publisher will be paid 100% effective in the quarter that BMI received Mary's notice.

Arrangements of Public Domain Works

Copyrighted arrangements of works in the public domain (classical and popular) will be credited at 20% of the otherwise applicable rate of payment for popular songs for all performances, with the exception of the Live Classical Concert distribution, where no payment is made for performances of arrangements of public domain works.

BMI Live

In our continuing efforts to ensure that songwriters performing in live music venues receive royalties at every stage of their careers, BMI has launched BMI Live, a program enabling those songwriters to register their concerts and set lists online to be considered for payment. To qualify, songwriters need to register their live musical performances on BMI.com/live. BMI will pay royalties to both writers and publishers via direct deposit. The distribution from BMI Live will be made quarterly; updates on the program are available on the BMI Live page.

Movie Theaters

U.S. movie theaters are exempt from the requirement of obtaining a public performance license and no one gets paid when songs are played in movie theaters for the public performance. The writer and sound recording owners, though, would be paid for the song's use in the movie. However, royalties are generated for foreign movie theaters, and for an international hit, it could add up to be some major cash.

Conclusion on Live Performance Royalties

Every songwriter or publisher should join either BMI or ASCAP. In theory, even if you are an unknown songwriter and play out live, you should collect royalties from playing your songs, and be sure to let your PRO know where and when you are playing. Now, I have been told by a former attorney for one of the two major PROs that they do not pay much, if any, money to independent songwriters for the live performance of their songs because their formulas for distributing royalties are based upon radio airplay and chart positions. SESAC is much better, and markets itself, as collecting live performance royalties for independent songwriters and publishers.

If you are a business, make sure you have a license if you play live or recorded music. If you get a cease and desist letter, then settle by just getting a license—they rarely seek retroactive damages and even more rarely sue the business. It's all negotiable. Some live music venues think they are getting around this by banning covers. This is insane. First, there's no way to enforce this as there are millions of songs and a performer could easily slip one it. Secondly, even an unknown songwriter can get paid their share.

Practice Tip: The only way of getting around it is to have a non-affiliated songwriter play only original material. This is very rare.

Chapter 12

● ● ●

TERRESTRIAL RADIO

Continuing with the duality theme of a lot of this book, there are, generally speaking, two forms of public performance: live and pre-recorded. Regarding the latter, there are two forms of radio—terrestrial and digital audio transmission. AM/FM stations (terrestrial) pay only the copyright holder of the song (the publisher). Digital radio (satellite, internet, cable TV) pay both copyright holders.

There are two ways for your music to get "radio" play:

1. The old-fashioned way: AM/FM radio where a "terrestrial" (meaning a broadcast tower) transmits your music to the world via good old fashioned radio waves.
2. And second, the new "Digital Transmission" way: for the most part, digital transmissions happen via the Internet (like Pandora or another Internet radio station); a satellite (Sirius Satellite Radio); or Cable TV (like Music Choice).

For example, Columbia Records negotiates a deal with Jeff Buckley to sing Leonard Cohen's song "Hallelujah." Columbia Records' version of the song is played on AM/FM radio. Cohen (the songwriter) gets paid for the public performance, but Columbia (Label) and Buckley (Performer) get nothing for this public performance. However, Columbia would be paid for the digital audio transmission which is the last right we will discuss later.

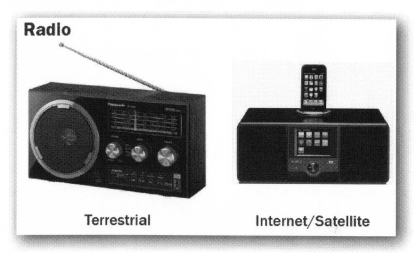

To even confuse the matter more, there are two kinds of digital radio: interactive (more like Spotify) and non-interactive (more like Pandora). I will flesh this out later, but generally with interactive steaming, a listener affirmatively wants to listen to a song or album by streaming it via an internet connection. This is more akin to a mechanical reproduction.[35] Non-interactive streaming is programmed for you so it is more like a radio public performance.

For terrestrial AM/FM radio play, every industrialized country in the world, EXCEPT the United States, requires both the Performer and Record Label to be paid when they play the song. Now, the record industry has introduced a bill in Congress called the Fair Play Fair Pay Act of 2015 to remedy this.[36] As you can imagine, radio stations are adamantly opposed to it, so I suspect it will not go anywhere soon. Most commercial radio stations in this country are owned by large companies such as Clear Channel and Cumulus.

It should be noted that terrestrial radio is starting to fade in prominence as more people switch to streaming or satellite. Plus, most commercial radio

---

35 Though to confuse even more, streaming sites like Spotify, also have radio components.
36 H.R. 1733.

plays few, if any, independent artists. In 2017, Norway will become the first country in world to turn off AM/FM radio; so, no more terrestrial radio there. We'll see if this becomes a trend.

Even though terrestrial radio does not pay the sound recording holder, they are trying to get rid of paying the PROs. The Local Radio Freedom Act (LRFA) is a "Sense of Congress" resolution trumped as supporting "small broadcasters" to what broadcasters claim is a performance "tax." This is a performance right that ensures music creators get paid royalties, and I doubt this will go anywhere as well.

Radio play is broadcast on federally regulated airwaves, so it is clearly a public performance. Because it is considered "promotional" they do not have to pay the master recording holder, just the publishers. So, radio stations, from commercial to NPR, must work out blanket license deals with BMI, ASCAP and SESAC to play music. A blanket license allows the station to play anything in the PROs catalog. Now, the PROs take this money and, after deducting their expenses, pass it on to publishers. While they do not reveal their exact formulas for this, I think it is fair to say that the major publishers get the lion's share of the money. Consult BMI's or ASCAP's website for further info on how they pay writers and collect from licensors.

The following is from BMI.com

Can I play my iPod in a bar?

Although most people buy digital audio files, CDs, or games like Guitar Hero thinking they are now their property, there is a distinction in the law between owning a copy of the music and owning the actual songs that are played. When you buy an audio file, software, or CD, even those specifically marketed for business purposes, the purchase price covers only your private listening use, regardless of how they are labeled. Once you decide to play any copyrighted music publicly, you need permission from the copyright owners.[37]

---

37 BMI contradicted this when I called them, and if the business has a license with them, I doubt they would care, though it technically may be a violation.

Aren't TV, radio and cable stations licensed with BMI already?

They are; however, those agreements do not authorize the performance of such TV, cable, and radio to the public by businesses and other organizations.[38]

Public performances of radio and TV are specifically addressed in Title 17, Section 110(5)(B) of the U.S. copyright law which states that any foodservice or drinking establishment that is 3750 square feet or larger, or any other establishment, other than a foodservice or drinking establishment, that is 2000 square feet or larger, must secure public performance rights for TVs or radios if any of the following conditions apply:

*   For TV, if the business is using:
    -   more than four TVs; or
    -   more than one TV in any one room; or
    -   if any of the TVs used has a diagonal screen size greater than 55 inches; or

---

38 There is an exception to this called the "homestyle exemption."
Exception for certain businesses paying PROs
1)Section 110(5) exemption ("homestyle exemption")
Section 110(5) of the Copyright Act provides an exemption for the reception of radio or TV broadcasts in an establishment open to the public for business. [v] The purpose of the "homestyle" exemption is to release from copyright liability anyone who merely turns on, in a public place, an ordinary radio or television receiving apparatus of a kind commonly sold to members of the public for private use. The basic rationale of this clause is that the secondary use of the transmission by turning on an ordinary receiver in public is so remote and minimal that no further liability should be imposed.

The exemption only applies to a single radio or television receiving apparatus of the type used in one's home. If the broadcast signal is received in an establishment of an area smaller than a certain gross square footage – less than 3,750 square feet for a foodservice and drinking establishment and less than 2,000 square feet for any other type of business – the law puts no limitation on the number of loudspeakers and TV monitors that may be connected to the receiving apparatus. [vi] Where the gross area of the business exceeds these minimums, the law imposes limits on the number of loudspeakers and TV monitors as well as on their placement and – in the case of audio-visual monitors – their size. The device must be relatively small and of limited sound producing capacity. In addition, the business may not directly charge customers for listening or watching the broadcasts and the signal may not be further transmitted. The broadcaster itself must be licensed by the Federal Communications Commission.

- if any audio portion of the audiovisual performance is communicated by means of more than six loudspeakers, or four loudspeakers in any one room or adjoining outdoor space; or
- if there is any cover charge.

* For radio, if the business is using:
   - more than six loudspeakers; or
   - more than four loudspeakers in any one room or adjoining outdoor space; or
   - if there is any cover charge; or
   - music on hold.

According to ASCAP:

"Most customers pay ASCAP an annual blanket license fee for the right to use any music in the ASCAP repertory. Some local radio and television stations opt for a per program license, under which they only pay ASCAP for programs containing ASCAP music not otherwise licensed. Every penny we collect, less operating expenses, is distributed to our members whose works were performed."

The case of playing music on so-called Internet radio (e.g. Pandora) likely falls outside the scope of the homestyle exemption. The language of the statute expressly limits the exemption to "a radio or television broadcast station licensed as such by the Federal Communications Commission." Internet radio transmissions, although seemingly fitting the same logic as radio and TV broadcasts over the air, do not require licensing by the FCC and are thus not squarely covered by the 110(5) exemption.

On the other hand, Pandora and other free Internet radio webcasters are usually licensed by the performing rights societies such as ASCAP and BMI and one could argue that the logic of the "homestyle exemption" should be extended to such radios as well. This argument, however, has not been tested in court yet and it is not clear whether courts would accept it. The safest course of action is to avoid playing Internet radio without authorization from the copyright holders.

An alternative to free Internet radio is satellite radio. In contrast to an Internet radio service such as Pandora, satellite radio subscription for businesses is covered by the homestyle exemption. SiriusXM for Business is a paid subscription service which handles copyright royalties for businesses. Through such a subscription, the business would avoid having to pay licensing fees to the different performing rights organizations. The business may choose to listen through an internet reception or through a satellite receiver. It should be noted, however, that the licensing fees for most performing rights organizations amount to an annual sum not substantially different than that charged by satellite radio. Depending on the negotiated price, a company may be indifferent between paying to one performing rights organization and subscribing to satellite radio. The advantage of a general license to play that society's repertoire regardless of the device chosen, e.g. personal computer or another audio system, may be overridden by the need to pay a licensing fee to several PROs, not just to one.

Where mom and pop stores play musical recordings, they engage in a performance of copyrighted material under the Copyright Act. If the music sound is clearly audible in the space designated for customers, the playing most likely infringes the owners' exclusive public performance rights in the sound recordings.

Pre-recorded music is ubiquitous. It pours from health clubs, gas stations, grocery stores, ballparks, and stores around the county. A PRO's customers are television broadcasters, including cable, commercial, non-commercial, and satellite radio, Pandora, Spotify, YouTube, Rhapsody, Netflix, Amazon and thousands of websites; colleges, concert and festival venues, symphonies, and hundreds of thousands of "general" licensees: bars, restaurants, hotels, ice and roller skating rinks, circuses, theme parks, veterans and fraternal organizations and more.

Businesses who run afoul of the PROs

This area is where attorneys most likely will run into music copyright law. If you have a client who has a bar or restaurant that hosts live music or plays pre-recorded music, you may get a cease and desist letter from the PRO demanding a payment and demanding the business obtain a license. PROs send agents out into the field to see if a business that does not have a license is playing music. There is no defense other than you are not playing music or meet the homestyle exemption. The business can play music in the back for staff if the customers cannot hear it. If you get a letter from a PRO, everything is negotiable in settling the case and even in the price of the license. For more on pricing, call BMI or ASCAP for a quote.

Failure to have a license is copyright infringement. The business may be subject to injunctive relief and substantial damages. The PROs could sue for either actual or statutory damages. A performing rights organization would likely sue for statutory damages as it would be difficult to prove actual losses and profits. The court has discretion to determine the amount of statutory damages in a range between $750 and $30,000 per individual copyrighted work infringed, i.e. for each song played. It must be noted, however, that a PRO will likely face challenging proof issues in identifying the pieces infringed. I will discuss damages more in Section Four.

Thus, when you see the words "All Rights Reserved" on a movie or music that you've rented or purchased, you know that playing that movie before a public audience is prohibited. The same restrictions apply to music that is purchased, broadcast, or live musicians that are hired to play in a public setting. Every business or organization must receive permission from the copyright owners of the music they are playing before playing it publicly.

Tracking of Public Performances

Kobalt, an independent publisher offering label services, is better than ASCAP, BMI and SESAC at tracking public performances. For example, ASCAP still uses a human "sampling" method, where someone listens to a radio station or sits in a store and writes down all the songs they heard for the afternoon, as old-fashioned as that sounds. If your music gets played on college or independent radio, you will probably fall under the sampling radar and will not get paid. BMI also uses sampling, but they say they use "performance monitoring data, continuously collected on a large percentage of all licensed commercial radio stations, to determine payable performances." They also use their "proprietary pattern-recognition technology." They call it a "census" and claim it is "statistically reliable and highly accurate." For college radio, BMI pays a minimum of 6 cents "for all participants."

Consent Decrees

Consent decrees are limitations agreed upon by parties in response to regulatory concern over potential or actual market abuses. BMI and ASCAP are essentially duopolies. Back in 1941, there was only one legally recognized copyright in music—the musical composition—and the balance of power in the industry was heavily tilted to the music publishers and ASCAP. At the time, ASCAP acted as a kind of gatekeeper to the world's most valuable musical repertoires, to the extent that the DOJ took action that same year to balance the scales. The result of this intervention was consent decrees that, to this day, govern how radio, whether AM/FM or digital, licenses compositions. BMI was placed under a similar set of conditions in the same year. ASCAP's consent decree was last updated in 2001; BMI's in 1994.

What do the consent decrees do? They are intended to promote competition in the marketplace for musical works, the consent decrees encourage ASCAP and BMI to compete with one another to attract licensees and recruit new songwriter/publisher members.

Under the consent decree provisions, ASCAP and BMI must offer licenses to services and venues on equivalent terms, although these licenses are non-exclusive and members of the PROs retain the right to individually license their works. For example, a radio station can pay for an ASCAP blanket license and play any composition in the ASCAP repertoire. Such licenses are available to AM/FM and television broadcasters, physical venues, and digital "radio" services like Pandora and SiriusXM. But if a songwriter/publisher wishes to negotiate a license for individual works outside of the blanket license and independently of their PRO, they are able to do so.[39]

---

39 If parties fail to come to agreement, licensees can petition the court. A federal judge in the Southern District Court of New York handles disputes and sets rates for a set term.

The consent decrees prohibit publishers from partially withdrawing just portions of their rights—such as those for digital transmission—from ASCAP and BMI. This means that the PROs administer all public performance rights for a given composition (including performance in AM/FM and TV broadcasting, digital broadcasting, and physical venues), or none of them.

Chapter 13

● ● ●

SYNCHRONIZATION LICENSING

This topic is important. Though it does not neatly fit into any area, it is good to talk about since we have covered most of the basic rights you get with a song. To use a song in a television show, movie, or commercial, you need permission from both copyright holders. You must obtain what is called a "Synchronization License" from the copyright holder of the song, and a "Master Usage" license from the record label (or whoever holds the sound recording). Sync for short, is the process of adding a song over any moving picture of any kind: TV, film, commercial, video game, and so forth. For instance, if a director wants to use a song such as Leonard Cohen's "Hallelujah," that was recorded and released on an album by Columbia Records, the director (or movie studio) must make a deal with both the songwriter for the song, in this case Cohen's publishing company, Sony/ATV[40]; and Columbia Records (for the recording of the song). He needs the publisher and Columbia Records to grant him the rights to both reproduce and distribute their copyrights. He does this by offering to pay them a lot of money (or other consideration, or maybe they give it away). These licenses grant the movie maker the right to reproduce and distribute the film with Columbia Records' recording of "Hallelujah."

---

40 A subsidiary of Columbia, which is a sub of Sony Entertainment.

Music used in TV and movies is not subject to a compulsory license, so publishers can charge what they can get for the song. There is no set rate, so it is whatever the parties can negotiate. Now, the television show, movie, or advertisement must get permission from both copyright holders because they are using both the song and the sound recording. Many new or unknown bands are using these avenues, perhaps without much payment, to get their songs in on the publicity. On the other hand, advertisers or big-budget movies can pay tens or hundreds of thousands of dollars to use a popular song in their creative work. If you get permission to use a song or re-recording of it in a film or movie, that does not apply to reproducing it in a video or DVD. You will need separate permission for that.

Practice Tip: If you cannot get permission from a sound recording holder, but have it from the publisher, you can always re-record (cover) the tune and use that version.

Some of you may be asking about the right to have the film shown on TV, and not infringe upon the copyright holder's exclusive rights to publicly perform the song or get paid for that performance. Well, those rights are negotiated with the broadcasters (i.e. the TV stations) on behalf of the copyright holders of the song by the Performance Rights Organizations via blanket licenses. So, the publisher would get paid for the public performance, but it is likely not going to be as much as the sync license.

Please note that if you want to use a song in a radio ad, there is no "syncing" the music with an image, so those are called transcription fees. Again, there is no set rate, you just negotiate, and certainly bigger acts have more leverage and can demand more because their songs are better known commodities. Also, keep in mind that these fees are usually split between the publisher and the record label, or whoever owns the music and sound recording copyrights, if they are different.

Major motion picture payments can run anywhere from $15,000 to $100,000, and up to $250,000 if the song plays over opening credits. Also, keep in mind that the terms of the license are what is important, and they usually include broad rights in all media in perpetuity. So, a movie studio can use a song in a trailer, boxed DVD set, and even prequels and sequels. This can be $25,000 or more. Now, a lot of films just use current popular songs to advertise the film, and the song is nowhere in the picture. This is basically like using a song in a commercial, and that can net $150,000 or more.

Obviously for independent films, the fees are much lower. If an indie film does not have a distributor, then the license can be around $500-$1500, and be limited to film festivals and for a one-year term. Now, you can have built-in escalators that match its release in theaters. It is possible to get a cut of the film in lieu of payment, though that is likely risky since a lot of films do not net money, at least on paper using strange Hollywood accounting. I would insist on a percentage of gross revenue.

A basic TV deal could be for over-the-air or cable TV, and options for more money if it is on a paid network like HBO. There could also be options for DVD or streaming services like Netflix, although shows are now being distributed exclusively online in venues like Netflix and Amazon Prime. Now, if a publisher originally licensed a song for over-the-air-TV, that would not necessarily include things like streaming on Hulu, so that license would have to be separately negotiated. This is the reason that some shows take years to get to DVD, like China Beach, and some never do. Shows like "WKRP in Cincinnati" had to replace some of the songs in the DVD that were originally broadcast because they could not get the license. Thus, new TV licenses are in perpetuity and include all forms of media (and probably those we have not even thought of or been invented yet).[41]

---

41 See AL KOHN &BOB KOHN,KOHN ON MUSIC LICENSING 329 (4th ed. 2010) ("Kohn") (stating that "[a]nyone who regularly seeks to clear licenses for the use of music in motion pictures, television programs, or advertisements should be quite familiar with . . .. one of the most frustrating barriers to clearing licenses: locating and obtaining permission from each of the several owners of the copyright"); Frequently Asked Questions: Mechanical, Synchronization & Other Licensing, SESAC, http://www.sesac.com/Licensing (stating that licensees need to contact all of the publishers or their administrators of a song in order to obtain a synchronization or mechanical license); see also National Music Publishers' Association ("NMPA")Jointly OwnesWorks Comments at 7 (stating that the "system of fractional licensing is consistent with how all music markets work, from synchronization rights to lyric rights to performance rights"); Donald S. Passman of Gang, Tyre, Ramer & Brown, Inc. on behalf of NMPA ("Passman/NMPd ")

TV deals can net anywhere from $10,000 to $50,000+, depending on the song. Out of context uses can yield up to $5,000 per week as long as the ad promoting the show is running. The singing shows such as *American Idol* only pay for what they use. These shows pay a set rate per song since they do not want to negotiate them separately, and they get good deals since publishers want the huge exposure these shows give the song.

For commercials, the range is anywhere from $50,000 to $200,000, or even in the millions if the song is iconic enough. Again, new bands or artists may license their songs for much less to get the exposure. When Microsoft used the Stones' song "Start Me Up" to launch Windows, they purportedly paid the Stones $7 million. Remember, Mick did go to the London School of Economics.

My sons both play video games and I am amazed by how many big songs from multiple genres and years are in those games. The fees are usually flat and can range from zero to $50,000 or more. Most deals are in the $5,000 to $10,000 range though.

In the major label world, the publisher, the songwriter, and the owner of the master recording will likely all be different entities. If you're in the independent music world, it's likely that YOU are all three people in one. So, licensing companies are helping independent artists get high paying syncs on TV and in film. Independent admin publishing companies like SongTrust, CD Baby and TuneCore are collecting royalties previously only available to those with publishing deals. YouTube is now offering a tip feature on channel pages and Spotify has integrated merchandise to artist profiles (without taking a cut).

Here is a list of some of the larger independent licensing companies for DIY artists:

Secret Road
All Media
Cellar Music
The Music Playground
Razor and Tie
Big Yellow Dog

Words and Music
Catch the Moon Music
Grand Rights—Music from Musicals and Operas

Below is a screenshot from CD Baby that also offers sync licensing.

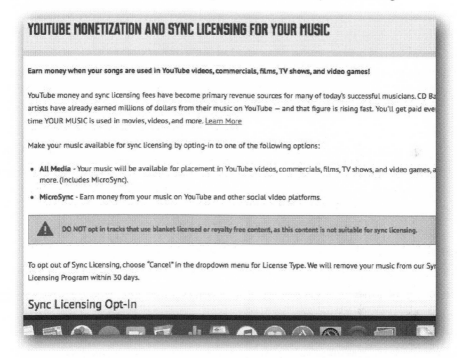

The PROs do NOT collect public performance royalties for dramatic musical works, what are sometimes referred to as Grand Rights, though that phrase is not in the Copyright Act. Dramatic works are generally works that tell a story such as plays, operas, and ballets. Authorization or licensing for these works can only be done through the copyright owner, usually either the creator or the creator's publisher. As you might guess, there's no set fee. You must negotiate with the rights holder.

There are generally two types of grand rights. First, works conceived to tell a story with music such as a play or musical. Second, there is use of an existing or commissioned work essentially used in a derivative fashion such as choreography or as part of a play.

Because the PROs acquire, and in turn license only, small or non-dramatic performing rights as distinguished from grand (or dramatic) performing rights, the distinction between a grand and small performance is crucial to determine whether a license from a performing rights society will authorize a given performance. The former General Attorney for ASCAP, Herman Finkelstein, has characterized non-dramatic performances as "renditions of a song . . . without dialogue, scenery or costumes." This characterization, however, appears both to be too broad and too narrow. It is too broad in that there may be performances devoid of dialogue, scenery and costumes, which are nevertheless dramatic.[42]

Here is an official ASCAP view (at least with respect to television performances) that the accompanying dialogue, scenery or costumes must help to carry forward the plot or "tell the story" in order to characterize the performance of a song as dramatic. This same rationale applies to licensing songs for use in TV shows, commercials and movies for much the same reason.

Political Ads

I get asked about this a lot, particularly in election years, especially presidential ones. Generally speaking, a live performance on television does not require permission and the network would pay the PRO a set prime time public performance fee for each and every live televised use of the song. The same is true if you are playing songs at a rally prior to the candidate coming out. Certainly, putting a song in a political ad would trigger the licenses we talked about above, but what about Donald Trump walking out to Queen's "We Are the Champions" at the Republican National Convention? Queen's guitarist Brian May was not thrilled, but what can he do about it? While the arena certainly has a public performance license with the PROs to cover the public performance of that and many other songs played there, clearly Trump's image was synced to the song and that image was transmitted live and may still likely be on the Internet.

---

42 Finkelstein, The Composer and the Public Interest—Regulation of Performing Right Societies, 19 L. & Contemp. Prob. 275, 283 n.32 (1954).

Thus, I would argue that the candidate in that circumstance would need permission from both rights holders. Now, they usually do not get it, and I have not seen any case law on this because elections come and go, and the use is usually fleeting.

Usage in Movies/Television/Commercials

Permission is needed from BOTH rights holders

When song is used in movies/TV/commercials, both copyright holders get paid, so record label and publisher would split income.

No set rate - just negotiate

Chapter 14

● ● ●

THE RIGHT TO PREPARE DERIVATIVE WORKS 17 U.S.C. 106(2) APPLIES TO BOTH COPYRIGHTS

A songwriter has the "right to prepare derivative works based upon the copyrighted work." This is the right to rip yourself off basically. If you write a poem, you can turn that into a song; a play becomes a movie; or a book a play, and so forth.

A "derivative work" is a work based upon one or more pre-existing works, such as a translation, musical arrangement, dramatization, fictionalization, motion picture version, sound recording, art reproduction, abridgment, condensation, or any other form in which a work may be recast, transformed, or adapted. A work consisting of editorial revisions, annotations, elaborations, or other modifications which, as a whole, represent an original work of authorship, is a "derivative work."[43]

The easy part of the right, also called the right of adaptation, is when the person creating the derivative work created the original one. So, if I write a song, I can change the lyrics or any aspect of the sound recording—make a dance mix or alternate version. The increasing more typical case though is where a musician uses another's song or sound recording in their new recording. Regarding songs, there are mainly two types: sampling and replay. Most

---

43 See 17 U.S.C. 101.

of the time you will just hear the generic term "sampling" to refer to either but there is a difference, and I will explain it below.

Section 103(a) provides that derivative works are protectable under Section 102. In theory, all works are derivative since they are derived from pre-existing works. This is especially true in music, which builds upon prior genres, styles and songs: African chants begat blues, which begat rhythm and blues; Celtic begat bluegrass which begat county and western swing; and, all of that begat Rock n' Roll. A work is not derivative unless it substantially copies from a pre-existing work.[44] Put another way, it would be an infringement if you did not get permission from the copyright holder of the pre-existing work.

A compilation of pre-existing works can be copyrightable also under Section 103. This means a collection of pre-existing songs can be copyrights as a collective work. This differs from a derivative work, where there is recasting or transformation. A soundtrack can be a compilation of songs already recorded; but a Spanish version of all those songs is a derivative work.[45] Any publication of a derivative work also, by implication, constitutes a publication of the underlying work on which it is based.[46]

Sampling

Sampling is the use of the actual master or sound recording in a derivative work. With the advent of home recording and digital technology, it became as easy as copying and pasting a legal document to lift a sample from one song to another. In the early days of digital sampling, there was no settled law and artists freely copied others' samples. The law eventually caught up. A couple of the seminal cases in this area are Grand Upright Music Ltd. v. Warner Bros. Records, Inc.,[47] and Bridgeport Music, Inc. v. Dimension Films.[48]

---

44 Nimmer at 3.01.

45 See Nimmer at 3.02.

46 See Nimmer at 4.12.

47 780 F.Supp. 182 (S.D.N.Y. 1991).

48 383 F.3d 390 (6th Cir. 2004).

The Grand Upright case involved Biz Markie's use of Gilbert O' Sullivan's "Alone Again, Naturally." Now, Markie called his song the same thing, and while you generally cannot copyright or trademark a song title, if you are going to rip someone off, you may want to change up the title a bit. Biz Markie used the same piano loop as O'Sullivan and even the same melody in the chorus. The first four words of the Judge's decision were "thou shalt not steal," so it was not a good day for Mr. Markie and his record label, Warner Bros.

The Bridgeport court held that any sampling of a master, even if unrecognizable, is a copyright violation. I do not know why you would sample something that is unrecognizable. But there is a very important distinction between the two cases: Grand Upright involved a musical composition, while Bridgeport dealt with the duplication of a sound recording. They both, however, set up a bright line or strict liability standard in using samples.

It should be emphasized that the defenses to sampling are different from a copyright infringement case.[49] The court in Bridgeport set about to establish a bright-line rule when it came to sound recordings, even very minimal use of sound recordings. In that case, only seven seconds or so of a master recording was used. The court found that any use of a sample from a master recording is a copyright violation, and there was no such thing as de minimis use. The court cited the language of 17 U.S.C. 114(b), and even a small part of a sound recording is something of value.[50]

Quoting the definition of a derivative work, sampling clearly involves "recast[ing], transform[ing], or adapt[ing]" one work in order to merge it with another work, the copyright holder of the work being recast, transformed, or adapted must generally grant permission for this to occur. Simply put,

---

49 Bridgeport at 396.

50 The court cited the below language in a footnote:

"(A)ll samples from a record appropriate the work of the musicians who performed on that record. This enables the sampler to use a musical performance without hiring either the musician who originally played it or a different musician to play the music again. Thus, sampling of records ... allows a producer of music to save money (by not hiring a musician) without sacrificing the sound and phrasing of a live musician in the song. This practice poses the greatest danger to the musical profession because the musician is being replaced with himself." Christopher D. Abramson, Digital Sampling and the Recording Musician: A Proposal for Legislative Protection, 74 N.Y.U. L.Rev. 1660, 1668 (1999) (footnote omitted).

because a sample is a derivative work, you generally cannot sample someone else's copyrighted work without permission.

Practice Tip: There is no set rate to clear samples, and you need permission from both copyright holders of a song. The permission is the same as using masters in commercials, TV shows, or movies.

For instance, if you want to sample the guitar riff from a Beatles' song, you would need to negotiate a deal with the copyright holder to the song (The Beatles' publisher), and negotiate a deal with the copyright holder to the version of the song from the recording from which you are sampling (The Beatles' record label, EMI). Either party can reject the request and refuse to grant you the right to create a derivative work.

Should they not reject the request outright, they will negotiate with you to attempt to come to terms that allow you to create a derivative work. Unlike mechanical royalties there is no legally required maximum rate for samples, so publishers and master sound recording holders will negotiate in order to get everything they can--including the rights to the copyright of the song that is using their sample.

Practice Tip: The three big major labels all have clearinghouses for samples to make money from another source.

Interestingly, there is a DJ called Girl Talk who crams hundreds of samples into one album and does not get permission to do so. I tell people, copyright violations are like speeding: we know what the law is, but we violate it a lot. Maybe Girl Talk figures it is easier to ask for forgiveness than permission.

Defenses to Using a Sample

Under the Grand Upright and Bridgeport decisions, the only real defense it would seem is that you did not use the sample. But there are a couple of options. While a long shot, you could argue that the sample was not original. Remember, only original material is subject to copyright protection.

Second, you could make the fair use argument of parody. We will discuss that later. Lastly, you could argue that your use was so minor as to not be an infringement.[51]

Bridgeport was squarely rejected by the Ninth Circuit in VMG Salsoul v. Ciccone.[52] "Other than Bridgeport and the district courts following that decision, we are aware of no case that has held that the de minimis doctrine does not apply in a copyright infringement case. Instead, courts consistently have applied the rule in all cases alleging copyright infringement. Indeed, we stated in dictum in Newton that the rule "applies throughout the law of copyright, including cases of music sampling." 388 F.3d at 1195 (emphasis added)." Indeed, no district court other than the ones in the Sixth Circuit have chosen to follow Bridgeport.

Certainly, major record labels were happy with the finding in Bridgeport because they own most sound recordings of major artists and must clear all usages. Artists and musicians, on the other hand, generally see this decision as stifling creativity and pricing them out from using samples.[53]

Thus, infringement takes place whenever all or any substantial portion of the actual sounds that go to make up a copyrighted sound recording are reproduced in phonorecords or by reproducing them in the soundtrack or audio portion of a motion picture or other audiovisual work.[54]

It should be noted that there is a difference of opinion as to whether the "substantial similarity" defense used in compositions applies to sound recording.[55] I think the only question is whether the sound recording was used, but I do think there should be a fair use test with that. Nimmer seems to think

---

51 While this is not a fair use defense, it does use one of the factors in fair use analysis. See 17 U.S.C. 107.

52 (9th Cir June 2, 2016).

53 See FROM MOZART TO HIP-HOP: THE IMPACT OF BRIDGEPORT V. DIMENSION FILMS ON MUSICAL CREATIVITY, UCLA Entertainment Law Review Winter 2007; BRIDGEPORT MUSIC'S TWO-SECOND SAMPLE RULE PUTS THE BIG CHILL ON THE MUSIC INDUSTRY CONFUSION IN THE DIGITAL AGE: WHY THE DE MINIMIS USE TEST SHOULD BE APPLIED TO DIGITAL SAMPLES OF COPYRIGHTED SOUND RECORDINGS, Texas Intellectual Property Law Journal Spring 2006.

54 House Report, p. 106, Nimmer 8.05, fn 13.

55 See Nimmer 8.05[A].

that if you alter a sound recording enough, that should part of the similarity test. The problem with that is you are still using the sound recording as the basis for the manipulation. Of course, you probably will not get caught since no one will recognize it, but it begs the question of why use it in the first place. To avoid legal issues, just create the sound you want to emulate.

Replay

This is the re-recording of a song or part thereof (a vocal or instrumental riff). You must get permission only from the songwriter, not the owner of the sound recording because you are not using the actual sound recording.

Practice Tip: If you cannot clear your sample, or it is too expensive, just re-record it if you get permission from the publisher.

Replay (or re-recording) is where a derivative work is created and used as part of another work via a re-performance/re-recording of a piece of the original work. For instance, if an artist, instead of taking the sample of a guitar riff from a Beatles' record plays the riff herself and then uses her version within her own song, she creates a derivative work of the composition (the song), but not the master.[56] In this situation, the person creating the derivative "replay" would need to negotiate a deal with the copyright holder of the song (i.e. the publisher), but not with the copyright holder of the recording (typically, the label). Of course, the publisher can reject the request, in which case the replay cannot be used.

"Thus, it seems like the only way to infringe on a sound recording is to re-record sounds from the original work, which is exactly the nature of digital sound sampling. Then the only issue becomes whether the defendant re-recorded sound from the original. This suggests that the substantial similarity test is inapplicable to sound recordings."[57]

---

56 Although she is re-creating what she hears from the sound recording.

57 Jeffrey R. Houle, Digital Audio Sampling, Copyright Law and the American Music Industry: Piracy or Just a Bad "RAP"?, 37 Loy. L.Rev. 879, 896 (1992).

If the publisher rejects you, then you can change the riff enough that it is your creation. Remember, it is not copyright infringement to be inspired to create something.

Defenses for Unauthorized Replay

Defenses for using a replay can be the same as a copyright infringement case. In other words, you have never heard of the original (you did not have access to it), and/or there is no substantial or striking similarity between the songs in question. Although, if there is no similarity between the two riffs, it begs the question why someone would even use it. You re-record samples because they are recognizable. We will discuss copyright infringement in detail in Section Four.

The defendant in Grand Upright argued that his sampling was warranted because it was so rampant in the industry. This was not well-received by the Court. You can also argue that the original song was not "original" (just like in a sampling defense), but originality has a very low judicial bar. Put another way, it is not unlawful to copy non-copyrightable portions of a plaintiff's work because non-copyrightable elements must be factored out in an inquiry into infringement.[58]

You may also attempt the fair use argument. The good news is that Fair Use is powerful defense. The bad news is that in order to assert it you have to have been sued and in trial. Further, there's no "bright line" in most cases as to what is "fair use." Fair use started out as a common law defense, but has since been codified in Section 107. Fair use is just an allowed transformative use as I discuss below.

The problem is that, absent parody, I could find no cases that upheld a fair use defense for using a replay without permission. The result is a world where copyright owners have the power to quash sampling or replay, should they choose to exercise it, though it is increasingly hard to police infractions

---

58 See Warner Brothers v. American Broadcasting Companies, 720 F.2d 231, 240 (2d Cir.1983) ("a court may determine non-infringement as a matter of law on a motion for summary judgment ... [when] the similarity between two works concerns only non-copyrightable elements of the plaintiff's work....").

with so much music being sampled as replays. It has led to a world where if you are a major artist, you will clear all samples and replays, and, if you are on your own, you likely will not and hope you do not get caught. The lack of case law may be because if a case goes to trial and appeal, there is likely a lot of money involved, which would preclude a fair use defense. While fair use is not used, as I mentioned above when discussing sampling, you can argue the use is so minor as to not amount to infringement as Madonna did successfully with her song "Vogue."

Mere similarity due to imitation will not establish infringement. Section 114(b) goes on to provide that the right of reproduction does "not extend to the making or duplication of another sound recording that consists entirely of an independent fixation of other sounds, even . . . though such sounds imitate or simulate those in the copyrighted sound recording." This copyright limitation has given rise to a genre of "sound-alike" recordings.[59] You can run into infringement issues, though, when you copy something into a new work.[60]

Using others' songs in yours

Sampling:
you need the permission of both the © and ℗ rights holders

Replay:
only need the permission of the © rights holder

---

59 See, e.g., Fantastic Fakes, Inc. v. Pickwick Int'l, Inc., 661 F.2d 479 (5th Cir. 1981).

60 A lot of songs (maybe most) are "inspired by" or "based on" copyrighted works, and, technically could constitute a "derivative work." But, unless the song is substantially similar to the preexisting work, a plaintiff will not be successful. Alcatel USA, Inc. v. DGI Techs., Inc., 166 F.3d 772, 787 (5th Cir. 1999) (Treatise cited). See Sweet v. City of Chicago, 953 F. Supp. 225, 228 (N.D. Ill. 1996) (Chicago's "Eat Your Art Out" sidewalk art fair does not constitute a "derivative work" of plaintiffs' "Eat Your Art Out, Chicago" guidebook).

Transformativeness and Parody

"[T]he ultimate test of fair use . . . is whether the copyright law's goal of 'promot[ing] the Progress of Science and useful Arts' would be better served by allowing the use than by preventing it."[61] Accordingly, fair use permits reproduction of copyrighted work without the copyright owner's consent "for purposes such as criticism, comment, news reporting, teaching (including multiple copies for classroom use), scholarship, or research."[62] The list is not exhaustive, but merely illustrates the types of copying typically embraced by fair use.[63]

Perhaps the only hole in the fair use argument, is parody. A lot of musicians think that if they transform a song or sample enough, then it is fair use. While the new work is entitled to copyright protection, just transforming a work that is not yours is not lawful. An exception to this is where the new version of the song is so different from the original so it is not a cover, or it is parody.

Practice Tip: I get asked about "transformativeness" a lot and I think it is very misunderstood. Just "transforming" a song or sample is not enough to avoid infringement.

The seminal parody case is Campbell v. Acuff-Rose Music, Inc. (the 2 Live Crew case).[64] The band 2 Live Crew used a sample of the Sony/BMG controlled master from the Roy Orbison song controlled by the publisher Acuff-Rose "Oh, Pretty Woman" in their song called "Pretty Woman." Campbell asked the record label for permission, but was refused. They remade the song anyway, giving credit to Orbison and the record label. The label sued, and the case made it to the US Supreme Court.

The Supreme Court held in Campbell, that while 2 Live Crew's unauthorized use of elements of "Oh, Pretty Woman" constituted a derivative work, the

---

61 Castle Rock Entm't, Inc. v. Carol Publ'g Grp., Inc., 150 F.3d 132, 141 (2d Cir.1998) (quoting U.S. Const., art. I, § 8, cl. 8).

62 17 U.S.C. 107.

63 Castle Rock Entm't, Inc., 150 F.3d at 141.

64 510 U.S. 569 (1994).

infringement was defensible as fair use because 2 Live Crew's version provides new insight to listeners, and thus represents socially important commentary. The Court compared the song to the original before applying the four-step analysis of Fair Use. The justices decided that the 2 Live Crew version "commented on" the earlier song and seemed to criticize it. They said that part of the content, along with the original rap lyrics, parodied the Orbison song. The court reached a unanimous decision that parodies fell under the fair use defense. See more in the Fair Use section later in the book, particularly the "Weird Al" discussion. Obviously, if you are going to parody something, you must refer to it, or, in this case, use the song they were parodying.

"Bittersweet" Revisited

If you listen to Andrew Loog Oldman's orchestral version of "The Last Time" by the The Rolling Stones and the Verve's "Bittersweet Symphony," you will note that the stings, which are the hook in "Bittersweet," are clearly re-recorded. Note that it is often hard to tell what is a sample from a master recording and what is a replay. In a lot of cases, you would need someone under oath who was at the recording. With technology advances, this only gets harder.

Given that the sample is likely a replay, the Verve only needed to get permission from the publisher of the tune, not the sound recording holder. So, they sought permission from the wrong entity. Now, there's no set rate for using a replay, but clearly giving up the whole copyright, especially when Richard Ashcroft wrote his own lyrics, is giving away too much. There's more similarity between the Stones' song and what inspired it— "This May Be the Last Time" by the Staple Singers—than the Verve's "Bittersweet Symphony." Alas, the song's title is but a cruel irony now. Another huge mistake they made is that they waited until the song was a massive hit in the U.S. before they sought permission from the U.S. publisher.

Conclusion

Get clear samples and permission from BOTH the copyright holder of song and sound recording. There is no set rate to use the sample. You just have to negotiate the rate, much like you would if you were going to use a song in a movie or commercial. All three major record labels have sample clearing-houses to make this process easier, and to take advantage of this growing area.

Under the adaptation (derivative) right, the copyright owner may prevent any unauthorized "translation, musical arrangement, dramatization, fiction-alization, motion picture version, sound recording copying, art reproduction, abridgment, condensation, or any other form in which [the] work may be recast, transformed or adapted."[65]

There are three routes to obtaining permission for a sample or replay if you are the party seeking to acquire the rights:

1. Work made for hire;
2. Obtain a license;
3. Buy the rights from a production music library (like a stock photo store) or Creative Commons.

Record labels and publishers have made it easier to clear samples, likely because this is another potential source of revenue for them, especially labels who own their own publishing arms. For example, Universal Music and BMG Music (two massive companies) now have online clearance houses at universalmusic-publishing.com and bmgmusicsearch.com respectively. Clearing samples can be time-consuming, so there are companies that do this for you called music clearance companies. Do an online search to find such companies.

One publisher/record company has even announced a sampling amnesty. From September 1, 2015, any artist who has used a sample from EMI Production Music division and Sony/ATV—the library music arm that con-trols both the composition rights and the sound recordings to a vast number of musical works will have a 6-month window in which they can step forward and hold their hands up. Sony/ATV will then do a licensing deal, at current market rates (whatever that might be), for future exploitation of the works, but, crucially, it will not seek retroactive royalties for past sales or exploita-tions, no matter how many years back they might stretch.

---

65 17 U.S.C.101 (definition of derivative works).

Simply put, because a sample is a derivative work, you cannot sample someone else's copyrighted work without permission. There is no such thing as a "small enough" sample, and the courts do not view ignorance as a defense. However, if you can show that there was no knowing or intentional infringement, the damages will be less than if you intentionally and knowingly infringed.

The terms of the license are the key. Is it worldwide? What types of distribution are covered? If you are an artist seeking a license, you want it as broad as possible. As I stated above, there is no set rate. George Clinton was paid $100,000 by De La Soul to sample his song "Knee Deep" in their song "Me Myself and I." Again, it is a matter of leverage. how famous is the song and songwriter and how much money does the licensee have? Another option is to make the licensor a co-writer to give them a percentage of the publishing. There are some rap or hip-hop songs with dozens of writers listed.

Chapter 15

● ● ●

THE RIGHT TO PUBLIC DISPLAY 17 U.S.C. 106(5) APPLIES ONLY TO SONG COPYRIGHT LYRICS

A creator gets the right to publicly display their copyrighted work. This right is more applicable to paintings, photos and like works, but, regarding music, it applies to lyrics, album covers, music videos, and marketing designs (though they're usually trademarked). You cannot display a song or sound recording, but only the physical embodiment of it. That would be the album cover. If you are on a major label, they will likely own the album artwork, but if you are an indie artist, you will. The same holds true for music videos, which are "other audio-visual works" protected under copyright law.[66]

Practice Tip: A band or artist is a brand and the product is more than music.

Regarding lyrics, a website that publishes song lyrics must get permission to display the words. The display (and, of course, reproduction) of song lyrics on a t-shirt, book, or a website can only occur if the copyright holder has granted the right.

This same right needs to be negotiated and granted to anyone that wants to create, distribute and/or reproduce sheet music. You generally need

---

66 17 U.S.C. 102(a)(6).

permission to reproduce lyrics, although there are many websites who violate this. Gracenote.com allows people to license lyrics from most of the major music publishers, much like Harry Fox does for mechanical licenses for covers. Increasingly, this right to display comes into play with respect to online lyric/tab sites.[67] It is unlikely that these websites that make money via advertising have negotiated with the copyright holder to display their lyrics. In other words, they are making money through advertising off other people's copyrights.

Music lyric sites are no small thing: Rap Genius has raised $15 million in venture capital and Kanye West is a fan, but they never obtained permission to post lyrics, and they were sued by the National Music Publishers Association (NMPA) in late 2013. The site has subsequently signed a licensing deal with Sony.

There is no set rate for lyric reproduction. You just need to negotiate one with the publisher. Interestingly, the compulsory license you get with a cover under Section 115 does not include the right to reprint lyrics in liner notes (if anyone still does that).

Lyrics

Lyrics and music to a song are the archetype for "interdependent" parts. Without the music, the song lyrics lose much, if not all, of their impact. Without the music, the lyrics are a poem. Judge Learned Hand observed:

> The popularity of a song turns upon both the words and the music; the share of each in its success cannot be appraised; they interpenetrate each other as much as the notes of the melody, or separate words of the `lyric.' ... To allow the author to prevent the composer, or the composer to prevent the author, from exploiting that power to please, would be to allow him to deprive his fellow of the most valuable part of his contribution; to take away the kernel and leave him only the husk.[68]

---

67 Tab sites give guitar or piano players the chords to a song.

68 Edward B. Marks Music Corp. v. Jerry Vogel Music, 140 F.2d 266, 267 (2d Cir. 1944); see also Nimmer, § 6.02 at 6-5 ("A lyricist is not likely to invest the effort and time attendant to such authorship unless he believes that he will own something more than a poem.").

This is a good time to discuss if there is more than one creator, or if someone specifically writes the lyrics to a song. If words and music are integrated in a song, then unauthorized use of the words or music, without the other, is a violation of the entire work. Lyrics alone would fall under a literary work.[69] Now, if there is a poem that is adapted to a song, it is an open question as to whether the compulsory license of Section 115 would apply. There are no court cases on it. Nimmer speculates that they could remain separate as a collective work.[70] I think it would trigger Section 115. Certainly, the new work would be a derivative work. If someone writes the lyrics to a song, they own as much of the song as the person who wrote the music. There is no such thing as a lyricists' share. Similarly, if you want to use someone's lyrics, you need to seek permission from the publisher, not just the lyricist. Of course, a songwriting team or group can have their own internal agreement between them as to how music royalties are split up between the different members.

The bottom line is to make sure that whomever you collaborate with, you are on the same page and that it is an equal contribution to the work, or that things equal out over several songs. The Beatles are a prime example of how a collaboration eventually wore thin. Most of their songs were credited as Lennon/McCartney. In the early days, they wrote together because they were constantly with each other. Both John and Paul contributed to songs like "I Want to Hold Your Hand". But, as the years progressed, and The Beatles stopped touring, they increasingly wrote separately more often. Thus, John would write "I am the Walrus" or "Strawberry Fields Forever" by himself, and Paul would write "Yesterday" and "Blackbird" alone.

This created problems and resentment, especially for Paul over the years. In the early 2000s, he came out with a book of poetry, and the lyrics to "Blackbird" were credited as Lennon/McCartney even though John did not write a single word. Similarly, the song "Yesterday" is co-credited even though Paul wrote the entire song, and John did not even play on the song. But that is the agreement they made early on, and it never changed. Paul even petitioned the British copyright officials to have his name put first on songs he alone

---

69 17 U.S.C. 102(a)(1); Nimmer 2.05[B].

70 See Nimmer 2.05[B].

wrote, and was denied this. Under British law, copyright authors are listed alphabetically (Jagger-Richards). Now, on his live album, "Back in the USA", he did list his name first on some songs. To hear him talk about this, find his interview on NPR's Fresh Air. Bottom Line: Once you wed lyrics to a song, that is how they are going to be credited, unless you copyright the lyrics before the song.

While there is no set mechanical rate for lyrics, here's a run-down of what it costs, or what publishers can earn, from lyrics:

* partial lyrics in a book or magazine is 1cent per unit, $200 minimum;
* longer excerpts can be as high as 4 cents per unit;
* lyrics for a paper greeting card run 12.5 to 15 cents per unit, or 5% to 8% of the wholesale price;
* lyrics for an e-card run 10 to 15 cents per unit or 5%- 8% of the retail price;
* if you play the song in a card, then it is usually what it would cost to use the master recording;
* lyrics on clothing are 8% to 11% of retail;
* most other products are around 6% to 8% of wholesale;
* lyrics for advertising is negotiable, just like if an advertiser wanted to use a song in a commercial.

Websites that print lyrics need permission to do so, and the publisher usually can get up to 50% of the advertising revenue.

Chapter 16

● ● ●

JOINT AUTHORSHIP

We have gone through five of the six exclusive rights you get with any song. We will review the last right in the next section where I discuss music copyright law in the digital age. Now that we have a framework for traditional music copyright law, we can delve into a few concepts that are key, but do not neatly fit into any specific area. This is a very important topic because, for example, in the year 2014, 93 of the top 100 charting songs had more than one writer.

Moreover, much contemporary music, particularly of the pop and urban genres, is created by assembling contributions from various sources—the "beats," "hook," instrumental track and melody (or "top line") may be sourced from different creators working independently, and combined by another author into a single work.

Section 201(a) of the Act states the obvious: "The authors of a joint work are co-owners of copyright in the work." Section 101 defines a "joint work" as "a work prepared by two or more authors with the intention that their contributions to be merged into inseparable or independent parts of a unitary whole." Thus, each contributor automatically acquires an undivided ownership in the entire work. So, two or more people work toward a predetermined common goal or design.[71]

---

71 See Nimmer 6.03.

The authors do not need to be physically together, in concert, have equal contributions in quality or quantity, or even have an agreement on joint authorship. The key is the intention of the authors. Indeed, in the digital age, you can write a song with total strangers from around the globe. Two cases illustrate this as it relates to music and lyrics. In the first case, a lyricist writes lyrics for a song. His publisher then shops the lyrics to a composer who turns them into a completed song. The court holds that the song is a joint work because at the time the lyricist wrote the lyrics, he intended them to be put to music, and the composer understood that as well.[72] In another case involving the song "Melancholy Baby," a husband wrote the music and his wife wrote the original lyrics. The wife's lyrics were rejected, and the husband consented to have new ones written. A court held that the new lyricist and the husband were joint authors.[73] Really, a joint work in theory is a derivative work because one author's contribution is transformed by another's. It is also like a collective work in that there is an assembly of separate parts to make a collective whole. Now, the big difference is that in derivative or collective works, the author only owns their contribution, whereas in a joint work each author owns an undivided interest in the whole work. How you label it depends on the author's intention when the work was created. This can be a big distinction. A screenplay to a movie is a joint work, while a movie based upon a play or novel is a derivative work. Admittedly, there is no bright line between joint authorship and a derivative work.[74]

A joint work is in theory broader than joint authorship.[75] Co-ownership of a copyright may also result from a transfer or (of)? inheritance. The theory behind joint authorship is that either the work by two or more people is so interdependent and intertwined that it creates one work. In writing a song, each person contributes lyrics and melody to a song. Or, you have a case where two or more independent parts make the whole, such as when someone writes

---

72 Edward B. Marks Music Corp. v. Jerry Vogel Music Co., 140 F.2d 266 (2d Cir. 1944).

73 Shapiro, Bernstein & Co. v. Jerry Vogel Music Co., 161 F.2d 406 (2d Cir. 1946).

74 See generally Nimmer 6.05.

75 See Nimmer 6.01.

the lyrics and the other person writes the melody as is the case with Bernie Taupin (lyrics) and Elton John (music).

Licensing and Derivative Works

Absent an agreement to the contrary, in a joint work, each author obtains an undivided ownership interest in the whole work, including, as such, "the right to use or license that portion of the joint work that was the sole creation of the other joint author."[76] This is the case even if the authors do not intend to create a joint work. For example, if someone writes lyrics, and then music is put to them, it is considered a joint work, and either one can license the complete work. The caveat here appears to be that either the lyricist or composer can license the lyrics or music separately without permission of the other.

What case law there is holds that these agreements must be in writing.[77] This is even more so given that copyright transfers must be in writing.[78] Unless written otherwise, the ownership interest of joint authors is that of tenants-in-common rather than a joint tenancy. Thus, the author's heirs will inherit whatever percentage the author had.[79]

Under the conventional doctrine of derivative and collective works, the owner of the underlying work retains her copyright, while the person who creates the new version may claim an exclusive copyright in that new version and his contribution, subject to his license to use the underlying work. The owner of the underlying work does not obtain any property right in the derivative (or collective) work, and likewise the owner of the derivative (or collective) work does not obtain any property right in the underlying work.[80]

Another consideration before you co-write with anyone is to make sure they are NOT signed to a publishing company. If they are, it makes things

---

76 Richlin v. Metro-Goldwyn-Mayer Pictures, Inc., 531 F.3d 962, 968 (9th Cir. 2008), cert. denied,555 U.S. 1137, 129 S. Ct. 1002, 173 L. Ed. 2d 293 (2009). See Nimmer 6.06.

77 Nimmer 6.08.

78 17 U.S.C. 204(a).

79 See Nimmer 6.09.

80 MCA, Inc. v. Wilson, 425 F. Supp. 443, 455 (S.D.N.Y. 1976) , modified, 677 F.2d 180 (2d Cir. 1981).

very difficult and will almost certainly prevent a licensing company from working with you and representing that song. Put something in writing that you have full rights and control over the song to license it without getting permission from your co-writers if they are affiliated with a publisher.

Practice Tip: Make clearing your songs for licensing as easy as possible for licensors if you have co-authors.

Contributions of Joint Authors

A contribution to a work is copyrightable if it (1) is independently created by the author and (2) possesses at least some minimal degree of creativity.[81] A person's contributions to a single work does not have to be equal in amount or quality, to qualify them as a joint author. But, such contribution must be more than de minimis. That is, a person must add more than a word, a line, a chord or note to qualify as a joint author.[82] There must be some intellectual contribution to be considered an author. You cannot claim authorship of an album if you just finance or make duplications of an album.

Regarding sound recordings, the sound engineer/record producer contribution was found to be that of an author.[83] This is not surprising given the Certificate of Registration you receive after your registration has been approved by the Copyright Office. On that form, under what the author created, there are five items if you copyrighted both the song and the sound recording:

1. Sound Recording
2. Performance
3. Production

---

81 See Feist Publ'ns, Inc. v. Rural Tel. Serv. Co., 499 U.S. 340, 345, 111 S.Ct. 1282, 113 L.Ed.2d 358 (1991).

82 Brown v. Flowers, 297 F. Supp. 2d 846, 852 (M.D.N.C. 2003).

83 Words & Data, Inc. v. GTE Communications Servs., Inc., 765 F. Supp. 570, 575 (W.D. Mo. 1991); Napoli v. Sears, Roebuck & Co., 835 F. Supp. 1053 (N.D. Ill. 1993), vacated, 858 F. Supp. 101 (N.D. Ill. 1994).

4. Music
5. Lyrics

The first three apply to the sound recording, while the last two the music composition. Clearly, production is a distinct part of a sound recording.

Practice Tip: With each item above, ask yourself who the author(s) and owner are.

There can be an issue because it is possible to copyright something as little as four or five notes, so the question of copyrightability comes up. Certainly, under the definition of joint authorship in the Copyright Act, there is no requirement that the contribution be copyrightable. So, you may have the juxtaposition that someone may contribute a copyrightable portion and NOT be a joint author, and someone contributing non-copyrightable things to a work and be an author. Now, it should be noted that contributing non-copyrightable ideas and getting authorship is not settled in the case law and the intention of the parties will usually govern.[84] You are more likely to see a non-copyrightable contribution as an author in the comic book or movie world than in the music industry, particularly regarding the composition.

If a band member contributes a line or two to a song, are they joint authors to the composition? What about all the chords to a song? It gets even more complicated with a sound recording beyond someone recording themselves in their home studio. Understandably, members of a band contribute to a sound recording, as does a producer and the performer or singer. While there is no bright line test, there are court cases that offer illumination.

In Aalmuhammed v. Lee,[85] the plaintiff had assisted Denzel Washington in his role as Malcolm X in the move of the same name. The plaintiff, a Muslim, had offered tips to the actors on the religion and its practices, and re-wrote a few scenes. He sued Spike Lee, the movie's director, claiming he was a joint author. In denying his claim, the Ninth Circuit wrote:

---

84 See Nimmer 6.07[A][3].
85 202 F.3d 1227 (9th Cir. 2000)

So many people might qualify as an "author" if the question were limited to whether they made a substantial creative contribution that that test would not distinguish one from another. Everyone from the producer and director to casting director, costumer, hairstylist, and "best boy" gets listed in the movie credits because all their creative contributions really do matter. It is striking in Malcolm X how much the person who controlled the hue of the lighting contributed, yet no one would use the word "author" to denote that individual's relationship to the movie. A creative contribution does not suffice to establish authorship of the movie.[86]

In Morrill v. Smashing Pumpkins,[87] the court enunciated a three-part test in finding that both the band and videographer were joint authors of a music video montage. In the absence of a contract, a person should be considered a joint author: (1) whether the purported author is "the master mind"; (2) whether the "putative coauthors make objective manifestations of shared intent to be coauthors"; and (3) whether "the audience appeal of the work turns on both contributions and the share of each in its success cannot be appraised."[88]

There is a case regarding the song "B.Y.O.B." by System of a Down. The song was actually registered as a joint work, and the court noted that "[a]n author's attribution of the work is "persuasive proof" as to whether the work was intended to be joint because the manner in which the parties "bill or credit" themselves is "a window [into] the mind of the party who is responsible for giving the billing or the credit."[89] Nevertheless, the court found this to be a mistake, and that one of the band member's contributions—a couple of phrases—was not enough to warrant being an author.[90]

---

86 Id. at 1232.

87 157 F. Supp. 2d 1120, 1123 (C.D. Cal. 2001).

88 Id. at 1123.

89 Maxwood Music Ltd. v. Malakian, 713 F. Supp. 2d 327, 344 (S.D.N.Y. 2010). (internal citation omitted).

90 Id. at 345-46.

Collective Works

Section 201(c) of the current Act expressly provides:

> Copyright in each separate contribution to a collective work is distinct from copyright in the collective work as a whole, and vests initially in the author of the contribution. In the absence of an express transfer of the copyright or of any rights under it, the owner of copyright in the collective work is presumed to have acquired only the privilege of reproducing and distributing the contribution as part of that particular collective work, any revision of that collective work, and any later collective work in the same series.

Agreements between Co-Writers

The co-authors of jointly created musical works often enter into agreements that define the percentages of copyright ownership of each co-author and provide that each will retain control over his or her "share" of the work. For example, a typical clause might stipulate that each contributor "shall administer and exploit only [his or her] respective ownership share" of the work. The "administration" of the copyright is commonly understood in the music industry to encompass the right to issue licenses and otherwise exploit the song and collect royalties from those uses.

What if the writers have different PROs? A typical clause stated that "the writers agree that they each shall separately administer their shares of the songs, [and] shall have the right to register the songs with their performing rights societies and to collect their writer's and publisher's shares of income directly from their respective performing rights society." Sometimes one co-writer may give the other, more famous co-writer complete say in licensing. That co-writer agreed to give his co-writers, each of whom also had a one-third share in the work, the "exclusive . . . right in perpetuity" to "[i]ssue and approve licenses" for the song. Again, as clearly permitted under the Act, this agreement supersedes what would otherwise have been the co-writers' presumptive equal interests in the copyright. Here, the co-writer relinquished the default right to grant nonexclusive licenses.

If you sign a publishing deal, you can only agree to whatever fractional percentage you own in the song—that is what your publisher would own (?). When a member writer collaborates with a writer who is a member of a different PRO, ASCAP and BMI generally make distributions only to their own member. In some instances, it could be difficult to ascertain whether a particular musical work is a joint work versus a derivative work or compilation without a full understanding of how it came to be created. The practice of fractional licensing represents an efficient solution to this problem as it does not depend upon the factual or legal assessment of individual works.

100 Percent Licensing

BMI and ASCAP are governed by consent decrees. The U.S. Department of Justice (DOJ) has recently proposed a rule whereby if one writer consents to a license to a song, the whole song must be licensed, regardless of the industry practice of fractional licensing where a licensee must clear it with all authors. Further, this would frustrate many agreements between writers.

While such a change as contemplated by the DoJ is welcomed by most who license music, the move away from the customary practice of fractional licensing, where each songwriter and/or its representative can only green light the use of their portion of a song, would cause a huge disruption in the industry, according to music publishers and songwriters, who express deep concern over the DoJ's interpretation.

The fallout from the Department of Justice's decision over U.S. consent decrees continues as this book is being published. In practice, this 100% licensing edict will mean that if a licensee clears a track with one writer/publisher, it will not need to bother doing so with his or her co-writers or co-publishers. This could give companies the power to shop around a track's multiple writers and rights-holders to get the cheapest deal.

The reality is that licensees in every other endeavor from synchronization rights, mechanical licenses, and print licenses live in a world of fractional licensing and have no problem securing licenses. In instituting this statutory reform, Congress intended that " [e]ach of the five enumerated rights may be subdivided indefinitely and . . . each subdivision of an exclusive right may be owned and enforced separately."[91]

For example, "[i]t is established law under the 1976 Act that any party to whom such a right has been transferred whether via an assignment or an exclusive license has standing to bring an infringement action based on that right," even when that party has been transferred only "a share of such a right."[92] As another example, where three songwriters collaborate on a single musical work, copyright law vests each songwriter with an undivided one-third interest in the copyright for the entire work.

Each co-owner may thus grant a nonexclusive license to use the entire work without the consent of other co-owners, provided that the licensor accounts for and pays over to his or her co-owners their pro-rata shares of the proceeds. A co-owner of a joint work may also unilaterally assign or exclusively license his or her own interest in the copyright, in whole or in part, to a third party, because to do so will not impair the rights of the other co-owners.[93] But a co-owner may not transfer the entire copyright, or grant an exclusive license to the entire work, as that would affect the rights of the other co-owners. Thus, a transfer of ownership or grant of an exclusive license can occur only through the signed, written agreement of all co-owners.[94]

Co-owners are free to alter this arrangement via a contract, and I think this is wise unless you agree with the default system. If you create song using samples or replay, absent an agreement to the contrary, you cannot license the derivative work without permission of the original work(s) used, unless they are in the public domain work unless there is an alternative legal basis to do so, such as that the original has fallen into the public domain. (sentence is weird)[95 ???]

---

91 H.R.REP.NO. 94-1476, at 61 (1976), reprinted in 1976 U.S.C.C.A.N. 5659, 5674 ("1976 House Report").

92 Minden, 795 F.3d at 1002-03; see also17 U.S.C. § 501(b) ("The legal or beneficial owner of an exclusive right under a copyright is entitled . . . to institute an action for any infringement of that particular right committed while he or she is the owner of it.")

93 Davis v. Blige, 505 F.3d at 99; Nimmer 6.11.

94 17 U.S.C. 204(a); Nimmer 6.07.

95 17 U.S.C.103(b) ("The copyright in a compilation or derivative work extends only to the material contributed by the author of such work, as distinguished from the preexisting material

A compilation is created when preexisting materials, which may constitute separate and independent works in themselves, are assembled into a new work of authorship.[96] As in the case of a derivative work, the copyright in a compilation extends only to the material contributed by the author of the new work, and does not include the underlying material. Accordingly, the creator of a compilation needs permission to license use of the work's constituent elements (again, absent other legal authority).[97]

In sum, absent a collaboration in the new work, the author of a derivative work or compilation does not share a joint copyright with the author of the underlying work(s), or vice versa.[98]

Whether the resulting work is a joint work as opposed to a derivative work or compilation cannot be determined without assessing the intent of the various authors involved in preparing their individual contributions, including whether they sought to merge them into "inseparable or interdependent parts of a unitary whole," as required under Section 101 of the Act. Thus, if ownership of a copyrighted work is divided among multiple parties, with each agreeing to license only his or her own share, a third party may face infringement liability if it uses a work without obtaining permission from all the owners.

---

employed in the work, and does not imply any exclusive right in the preexisting material. The copyright in such work is independent of, and does not affect or enlarge the scope, duration, ownership, or subsistence of, any copyright protection in the preexisting material.");

96 17 U.S.C. 101 ("A 'compilation' is a work formed by the collection and assembling of preexisting materials or of data that are selected, coordinated, or arranged in such a way that the resulting work as a whole constitutes an original work of authorship. The term 'compilation' includes collective works.").

97 See Tasini, 533 U.S. at 497.

98 For an excellent summation of these issues, see Copyright office memo on 100 percent licensing dated Jan. 12, 2016. Just do a search at copyright.gov.

Chapter 17

● ● ●

WORKS MADE FOR HIRE AND TERMINATION RIGHTS

This is typically referred to as works for hire, and this occurs usually when you hire someone to do a creative work, and you (the person who hires say a graphic designer) owns the work and not the person who created it. In the case of works made for hire, the employer and not the employee is considered to be the author. Section 101 of the Copyright Act defines a "work made for hire" as:

1. a work prepared by an employee within the scope of his or her employment; or
2. a work specially ordered or commissioned for use as:
    - a contribution to a collective work
    - a part of a motion picture or other audiovisual work
    - a translation
    - a supplementary work
    - a compilation
    - an instructional text
    - a test
    - answer material for a test
    - an atlas

The parties can expressly agree in a written instrument signed by them that the work shall be considered a work-made-for-hire.[99] With a work-made-for-hire, "the employer or other person for whom the work was prepared is considered the author for [copyright] purposes . . . ."[100] Under Section 101, "a work prepared by an employee within the scope of this employment" constitutes a work made for hire. Congress, however, did not define the terms "employee" or "within the scope of employment," so the U.S. Supreme Court has interpreted this to mean that the general common law of agency applies.[101]

It should also be noted that the law may be different if the work was created prior to January 1, 1978. So, there are two mutually exclusive ways to have a work-made-for hire: the employment relationship and as an independent contractor. "In determining whether a hired party is an employee under the general law of agency, we consider the hiring party's right to control the manner and means by which the product is accomplished."[102]

The factors enunciated in CCNV are applied like the factors laid out for fair use. The facts of each case determine which factors are more important than others. After the right to control, the CCNV factors are as follows:

> Among the other factors relevant to this inquiry are the skill required; the source of the instrumentalities and tools; the location of the work; the duration of the relationship between the parties; whether the hiring party has the right to assign additional projects to the hired party; the extent of the hired party's discretion over when and how long to work; the method of payment; the hired party's role in hiring and paying assistants; whether the work is part of a regular business of the

---

99 See Circ 1 from Copyright.gov.
100 17 U.S.C. 201(b).
101 Community for Creative Non-Violence v. Reid, 490 U.S. 730 (1989) (hereafter CCNV).
102 CCNV, 490 U.S. at 738-39.

hiring party; whether the hiring party is in business; the provision of employee benefits; and the tax treatment of the hired party.[103]

Even employees can claim copyrights in their work if it does not relate to the employment itself.[104] Thus, the literary efforts of an employee writing his novel over lunch, or a professor's notes of his lectures are generally going to be their creative work because they are not rendered within the scope of his or her employment. Further, if a work would not be regarded as falling within the employment relationship, just because a portion of it was done during work time is not dispositive. Conversely, work done at home that is related to employment may not necessarily be that of the employer. In other words, the employer does not own the brain of the employee simply because they are an employee.

There is a 3-part test under the Restatement of Agency as to when an employee's conduct is within the scope of his employment.

1. It is of the kind of work he is employed to perform;
2. It occurs substantially within authorized work hours and space;
3. It is actuated, at least in part, by a purpose to serve the employer.[105]

The above is true even if a contract says to the contrary. Thus, if an employer says that anything done at work is a work-made-for-hire, even if it falls outside the scope of employment, it will not necessarily be so (the same is true of a record company). Such agreements may be regarded as a transfer of copyright from the employee to employer, but not trigger the various consequences that stem from a work-for-hire situation. In other words, the copyright itself may be transferred to the employer, but it is not a work-for-hire. Regardless, in general, where there is an employment agreement, if it states the employer owns the copyright, the employee has a high burden of proof to show otherwise.[106]

---

103 CCNV, 490 U.S. at 751-52.
104 Nimmer 5.03[B][1][b][i].
105 Id.
106 Nimmer 5.03[B][1][b][ii], fn 98.1.

Therefore, under the current Act, not every work prepared by an independent contractor on special order or commission is a work-made-for-hire. Section 101 lists the categories of specially ordered or commissioned works. If the work does not fit into any of these specific categories, then it will not qualify as a work-made-for-hire.

Works-for-Hire in the Music World

As it relates to music, this can be an issue. Say you write a song and then hire, or most likely have friends who are musicians come over to flesh out what you have written. If you record all by yourself, this is not an issue, but most people do not. In the major-label world, this will likely be contractually spelled out; in the indie world, not so much.

Below is an excerpt from BMI.com. I have added what is in brackets:

Failure to Clarify Whether Musicians' and Vocalists' Contributions are a "Work for Hire"—or a Collaboration

It's critically important to communicate and delineate upfront whether a musician's or vocalist's contribution to your demo [or song/ sound recording] constitutes a collaboration—or is he or she being paid a flat fee, with no additional amounts to be paid, regardless of how the recording might be used.

Whether or not a musical contribution is deemed a collaboration is determined partly by the musical style. For example, it would be almost unheard of for professional musicians in Nashville to request a writers' credit when recording a country music demo—regardless of the extent of the suggestions or changes they might make, or the musical hooks they might add. It is understood that this is part of what they are being hired to do.

However, when working in pop, hip-hop, R&B, dance, rock, and other genres—and when working with friends who are not pro session players, and in cities other than Nashville—musicians' contributions may well be considered as collaborations. Drum beats, chord changes, guitar licks, synthesizer lines and bass riffs might all [potentially] earn writers' credits.

It's equally important to be clear about whether you have the right to include the singer or player's performance in a television show, movie or other media—and if so, whether they will be compensated.

Remedy: Prior to the session, clarify whether performances are to be defined as collaboration or as a "work-for-hire." If it is agreed that a performance is a work-for-hire, have your musicians and vocalists sign a "Work-for-hire Agreement" (aka "Musicians'/ Vocalists' Waiver").

If there is a possibility of placing your demo recording in a TV show or film, you might offer your vocalist and primary musicians a percentage of any master use license fee earned for the placement of the recording. However, it is important to note that musicians and vocalists in Nashville who are members of their respective unions are not permitted to sign "Work-for-hire" agreements when they perform on demos. Their compensation is determined by their union contracts. Your best protection is clear communication and obtaining signed agreements prior to the recording session.

Here's my take on works for hire v. collaboration. It would be extremely difficult for a musician to claim collaboration for "drum beats, chord changes, guitar licks, synthesizer lines and bass riffs" as BMI claims because all of those would be based upon, or derived from, my song, especially given that you cannot copyright common chord changes and most songs are built upon that. I agree you should be clear that the musicians are a work-for-hire, though if you want to kill the buzz during a recording session, just whip out a contract.

Practice Tip: Have musicians who come in to play your song waive all copyright in both the song and the sound recording.

For 99.9% of cases, this will not be an issue because the album or song will not take off, and many musicians understand that they did not write the song, they only played on the track. I have used many musicians on my albums and this has never been an issue. Some I have paid, and some I have not. With this in mind though, I will give you the following suggested agreement that a songwriter could use if you wanted to.

Work-for-Hire and Musicians' Waiver Agreement

I, [the musician] agree that any participation in this project/song/album is a work made for hire and not a collaboration, and that I am making a contribution to a collective work. I acknowledge that I have received compensation or consideration for my performance on this project/song/album and have no copyright interest in any of the songs or sound recordings, or in any copyright related to the song.

Further, if this Agreement is found by any Court or other jurisdiction to not be a work- made-for-hire as defined in 17 U.S.C. 101, then I hereby transfer any and all interest of my copyright in the song or sound recording to [NAME OF COMPOSER/OWNER.] My transfer and assignment is irrevocable and in perpetuity, and I hereby forever license my performance and/or production to [NAME OF ARTIST].

An example of a work-for-hire is the Budweiser commercial using a song of Dan Rodriquez titled "Friends Are Waiting." As of this writing, the spot has more than 19 million views on YouTube. It is in a commercial touting not to drink and drive. Well, it turns out that Bud hired Dan to do this as a work-for-hire and did not license the song. So, Bud just paid him (apparently a small amount) and can use the song as it wishes because Bub owns it. Rodriquez cannot sell the tune on iTunes and Bud has not given him much publicity. Now, Rodriquez, a Minneapolis musician, knowingly agreed to this, and still has gotten some publicity for this song that can help him in other ways, certainly.

Lessons for songwriters: Be careful and try to avoid giving your songs away via a work made for hire. Clearly, Bud has more power than an unknown singer/songwriter who is likely desperate for the publicity. If that's the only deal, try to get as much as you can for the work, or, better yet, just license the song.

Termination Rights of Sound Recordings

This is going to be a big area of law for musicians on record labels, and something to watch for. When copyright law was revised in 1976, musicians, like creators of other works of art, were granted "termination rights," which allowed them to regain control of their work after 35 years, so long as they apply at least two years in advance. Recordings from 1978 were the first to fall under the purview of the law, and became eligible in 2013, and 1979 works in 2014, and so forth. Thus, Congress passed the copyright law in 1976, specifying that it would go into effect on Jan. 1, 1978, meaning that the earliest any recording can be reclaimed is Jan. 1, 2013. But artists must file termination notices at least two years before the date they want to recoup their work, and once a song or recording qualifies for termination, its authors have five years in which to file a claim. If they fail to act in that time, their right to reclaim the work lapses.

With the major revision of the Copyright Act in 1978, Congress recognized the necessity of "safeguarding authors against unremunerative transfers ... needed because of the unequal bargaining position of authors, resulting in part from the impossibility of determining a work's prior value until it has been exploited."[107] The goal was to offer to authors a chance to reclaim their creations that they may have given away due to a lack of leverage in negotiations because they had no bargaining power.

The Copyright Act provides that, notwithstanding a termination of rights:

> A derivative work prepared under authority of the grant before its termination may continue to be utilized under the terms of the grant after its termination, but this privilege does not extend to the preparation after the termination of other derivative works based upon the copyrighted work covered by the terminated grant.[108]

---

107 H. Rep., p. 124. See Harry Fox Agency, Inc. v. Mills Music, Inc., 543 F. Supp. 844, 859 (S.D.N.Y.
1982), rev'd on other grounds, 720 F.2d 733 (2d Cir. 1983).
108 17 U.S.C. 203(b)(1), 304(c)(6)(A).

Regarding derivative works, a grant of composition rights in lyrics will authorize the preparation of a song based on the lyrics. Even after the statutory termination of that grant, the grantee will continue to have the right to "utilize" the film made pursuant thereto. But the grantee would not have the right, after termination, to prepare a new song based on the same lyrics.

If there are joint authors, a grant executed after Jan. 1, 1978, may only be terminated by a majority of authors. Before examining the meaning of "majority," it should be noted that a joint author may not "transfer" a greater copyright interest in a work than he owns. Thus, the author may transfer to another his share of the copyright and may grant a nonexclusive license in the entire work without the consent of any other joint author (subject to a duty to account to the non-granting joint authors).[109]

But the author may not grant an exclusive license of rights, nor may he transfer more than a proportionate interest in the entire work. When fewer than all joint authors are empowered to act as agents for all in making an exclusive grant of rights, such a grant should be considered as having been made by all joint authors for purposes of deciding who may terminate. If there are only two authors, then both would have to consent to termination.

Joint ownership of copyright is conceptualized as a tenancy in common. A tenant in common may grant non-exclusive licenses in the jointly authored work or may transfer his or her share of the tenancy in common (may sell or give away his or her share of the copyright). The tenant may not use the tenancy so as to exclude co-tenants from similar use (may not grant an exclusive license nor assign an exclusive ownership in the work).

Termination of grants executed on or after Jan. 1, 1978, may be "effected at any time during a period of five years beginning at the end of thirty-five years from the date of execution of the grant." Thus, for a grant executed on June 6, 1985, the first date on which it is subject to termination is June 6, 2020. The last date is June 6, 2025.[110]

---

109 17 U.S.C. 304(d) ("the exclusive or nonexclusive grant of a transfer or license of the renewal copyright or any right under it ... is subject to termination").
110 17 U.S.C. 203(a).

The provision also permits songwriters to reclaim ownership of qualifying songs. Bob Dylan has already filed to regain some of his compositions, as have other rock, pop and country performers like Tom Petty, Bryan Adams, Loretta Lynn, Kris Kristofferson, Tom Waits and Charlie Daniels, according to records on file at the United States Copyright Office.

Some artists will fight hard to reclaim what they probably thought was theirs all along. Don Henley, founder of the Eagles and the Recording Artists Coalition (which seeks to protect performers' legal rights), was quoted in the New York Times, "In terms of all those big acts you name, the recording industry has made a gazillion dollars on those masters, more than the artists have. So there's an issue of parity here, of fairness. This is a bone of contention, and it's going to get more contentious in the next couple of years."

Now, the labels are expected to fight hard claiming the artists' work was "made for hire." "We believe the termination right doesn't apply to most sound recordings," said Steven Marks, general counsel for the Recording Industry Association of America, a lobbying group in Washington that represents the interests of record labels. As the record companies see it, the master recordings belong to them in perpetuity, rather than to the artists who wrote and recorded the songs, because, the labels argue, the records are "works-for-hire," compilations created not by independent performers, but by musicians who are, in essence, their employees.[111]

While this question ultimately will be decided by the courts, record labels are going to have a very hard time proving that artists were employees or the sound recordings were "works made for hire." This is because under most (one-sided) record contracts, the costs of recording were fronted by the label and then recouped by them via record sales. In essence, the artist paid for the recording, and has much control over it, particularly if they wrote all the music. Quoting Don Henley again, "It's very simple: We created and paid for these records." It remains to be seen how the contributions of producers, engineers and other musicians are treated because they are, or can be, part of the sound recording.

---

111 See New York Times, August 16, 2011, p. C1.

Termination Rights: Are Sound Recordings a Work-for-Hire?

Note that sound recordings are absent from the definition of work-for-hire in Section 101. A sound recording can be fit in the definition as a supplementary work, collective work, or created by a salaried employee.

In 1999, Congress amended the work-made-for-hire definition, in a law unrelated to copyright law, to explicitly add sound recordings to the definition of a work-for-hire.[112] What Congress thought was merely a technical amendment clarifying the law as it was, instead created a firestorm in the industry. Congress scheduled hearings on the matter in front of the House Subcommittee on Courts and Intellectual Property.

The chair of the committee, Howard Coble, had noted that record companies had been registering sound recordings as works made-for-hire and had "inserted boilerplate language in all recording contracts which specified that the sound recording were works for hire." He noted that all artists, except for a very few, sign these work-made-for-hire agreements.[113] The chair also noted that no one had ever challenged a registration on the basis that a sound recording does not qualify as a work-made-for-hire.

The Register of Copyrights, on the other hand, noted that, while in the 1960s record companies did employ backup singers and engineers, today, "in many cases record companies simply provide funds at the front-end, and distribution at the back end of a sound recording's production."[114] Less than a year later, Congress repealed the addition of sound recordings as works-made-for-hire, going so far as to state that nothing should be read into making sound recordings as a work-for-hire for a brief time.

The record companies have another trick up their sleeve, however. The recording contracts typically state that if a court finds the artist's sound recording is not a work-made-for-hire, then the works are considered assigned to the record company. This type of clause is usually non-negotiable unless you are a popular artist with a lot of leverage.[115]

---

112 It was passed in something called the Satellite Home Viewer Improvement Act of 1999.

113 Nimmer 5.03[B][2][a].

114 Id.

115 See Tee Vee Toons, Inc. v. MP3.com, Inc. 134 F.Supp. 2d 546, 549 (S.D.N.Y. 2001).

So, what's the big difference if the record company owns the sound recording via a work-made-for-hire or simply through an assignment? A work-made-for-hire continues through the life of a copyright, while an assignment is subject to statutory termination of transfers. Plus, recording artists will be able to affirmatively terminate their contracts beginning in 2013, but only on the assumption that the sound recording is NOT a work-made-for-hire. In other words, if the sound recording qualifies as a specially commissioned work-made-for-hire, they are not subject to termination, otherwise, they are.[116]

The lobbying arm of the record labels, the Recording Industry Association of America (RIAA) argues that an album is simply a contribution of an individual sound recording as one of several selections on an album. Thus, it is a contribution to a collective work. There is no consensus on whether a sound recording is a collective work because some sound recordings are dependent on a producer, an individual, or a group. While Nimmer concludes there is no "arm chair answer," in most circumstances, with the artist or band writing the songs and doing most of the music, most sound recordings would not qualify as collective works. I agree with him that in most circumstances, absent, say a soundtrack or benefit album featuring multiple performers, sound recordings are not collective works.

Hence, there is a two-level inquiry: First, is it a work-made-for-hire (likely not), and, second, if not, does it fall within the Section 101 definition of a work-for-hire (again, probably not)? Assuming artists can terminate their sound recording contractual provision, this could jeopardize others' interests who also worked on the sound recording, like a producer. They can also terminate and claim ownership in the sound recording. Who is the real author here? There could be many people who could claim an interest.

In order to avoid the above scenario, the Copyright Office recommended the only key contributors be given the right of termination; not surprisingly, the record companies objected to this. Artists responded that side musicians, back-up singers and engineers are hired to work on a song with the contractual understanding through standard industry agreements that their contributions

---

116 Nimmer 5.03[B][2][a].

are made without any claims to authorship.[117] While this area still needs to be settled, one court has already concluded that "the only way that this can be a work-for-hire is if plaintiffs are employees of defendants."[118]

Even if the work falls within a special order or commission, it will not be a work-made-for-hire unless "the parties expressly agree in a written instrument signed by them that work shall be considered a work-made-for-hire."[119] There are generally no magic words, but courts look at the intent of the parties. No written instrument is required if an employee creates something within the course of his or her employment.

By the way, in a copyright transfer, only the owner of the copyright needs to sign the document transferring rights, not the one receiving those rights.[120] The writing should be done prior to the work beginning, but can be done after the work is completed if the agreement ratifies the understanding of the parties.[121] In determining whether a work is commissioned, the motivating factor in producing the work was the person requesting preparation of the work who induced its creation.[122]

The parties can by agreement vary the rights which would otherwise be owned by the employer, but they cannot change the "author" for copyright purposes.[123] This is to avoid the legal consequences of a work-for-hire, such as the length of copyright. The employer's transfer of a work-for-hire to the employee requires compliance with the specialized provision of Section 201(b), rather than the Copyright Act's general transfer provisions.[124]

In 2013, Victor Willis of the Village People (the Policeman) reclaimed his lost song compositions. Willis had co-written more than 30 songs for the Village People, including "YMCA." A federal district court in California found in his favor and did not buy the argument he was an employee. While

---

117 Nimmer 5.03[B][2][a][ii].

118 Buccharelli-Treger v. Victory Records, Inc., 488 F.Supp.2d 702, 709 (N.D. Ill. 2007).

119 17 U.S.C.101.

120 17 U.S.C. 204(a).

121 See Playboy Enters., Inc. v. Dumas, 53 F.3d 549 (2d Cir. 1995).

122 Playboy at 563.

123 Nimmer at 5.03[D].

124 See Nimmer 5.03[D].

this involved a music composition, I think the same result will hold true for sound recordings. Two side notes on this: Willis' wife is a lawyer and apparently alerted him that he could reclaim his rights, and he claimed in the New York Times he would consider blocking the current version of the Village People[125] from performing the song in public. While the plain language of Section 106(4) may support him, I do not know how this would be accomplished; I suppose an injunction. I have never heard of this being done and Willis would be forfeiting some public performance revenue.

Wrapping up Works-for-Hire, Termination Rights and Sound Recordings

Creators who have transferred their copyright can now attempt to reclaim their copyright 35 years after that transfer. This applies to all copyright, not just music. This was to protect artists who gave away their works for little (or nothing) and that work became well-known.

The only catch is there is no termination if the work qualifies as a work-for-hire under Section 101. The two ways a work-for-hire is created is by an employee during her employment, and works commissioned for independent contractors. There must be a contract, and it must fall in one of the following categories: (1) contributions to collective works; (2) part of a motion picture or other audiovisual work; (3) supplementary works; (4) compilations; (5) translations; (6) instructional texts; (7) tests; (8) answer material for tests; or (9) atlases. Really, the only possibility for music is contributions to a collective work. If it does not fit into any of these, then it is likely not a work-for-hire.

Another option for someone hiring a contractor to create a work is for them to just license it from the creator for a period of time. Certainly, the details of the license would be key, but this option helps both parties. The creator retains the copyright and the contractor gets use of the work per the license.

---

125 There are few, if any, former members in the recent lineup.

Chapter 18

●　　●　　●

WRAPPING UP THE EXCLUSIVE RIGHTS

The above five exclusive rights can be and often are transferred, at least in part. Or, at the very least, you give someone a non-exclusive license to one of them like when you hire someone to reproduce your CDs. Non-Exclusive transfers do not need to be in writing, but exclusive ones do. Copyrights are personal property rights and, as such, are governed by whatever jurisdiction you are in that governs those rights. Therefore, they can be transferred via a will.

The exclusive rights of reproduction, distribution, and adaptation (to make a derivative work), apply equally to both copyrights in a song. You can reproduce and distribute songs and sound recordings via phonorecords. You can make a derivative work of a song via a sample or replay; you can make a derivative work of a sound recording via a sample. The right of live public performance applies only to the song copyright. Only music lyrics can be publicly displayed.

The Cardinal Rule: "Do everything you can to control your copyrights and manage your own publishing company." --John Eastman, International Copyright Attorney, and Linda Eastman's father, advice to Paul McCartney.

Unfortunately for Paul, it was too late to heed that advice in the Beatles' era, but he certainly did later in his career.

Thus, for each copyright in the song, ask yourself the following:

1. Who owns the copyright?
2. Who collects the money?
3. How is the money divided?

SECTION THREE

● ● ●

MUSIC COPYRIGHT LAW IN THE DIGITAL AGE

Overview

In the early 90s, the advent of storing music in digital files on a computer, or smaller device such as an iPod, radically changed the music industry. Those changes are still being felt today. This section deals with terrestrial radio, digital radio, and the last right you get with a copyright.

We will discuss a host of topics ranging from file sharing and downloads to YouTube and the new model of music streaming. This area is ever-changing and can be complex. I have attempted to give you the most recent information I have in the simplest way without compromising the law.

The concepts of public performance and mechanical royalties do not easily fit into the digital age. Below is an illustration from Harry Fox indicating the complexity of this area. I will attempt to break this area down as simply as I can.

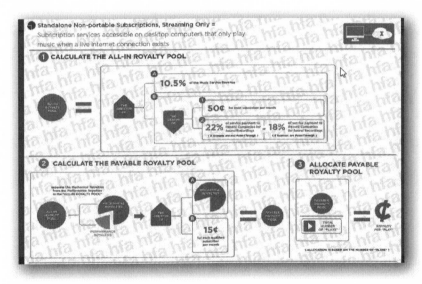

Chapter 19

● ● ●

THE RIGHT OF DIGITAL TRANSMISSION 17 U.S.C. 106(6) APPLIES ONLY TO SOUND RECORDINGS

The creator has the right, "in the case of sound recordings, to perform the copyrighted work publicly by means of a digital audio transmission." This right is just a subset of the Public Performance right, and was added to reflect the new technology that allowed digital transmission. By its very words, this right only applies to sound recordings. In the major label world, they would own these per the record contract. In the DIY world though, the band or artist would likely own their masters.

Practice Tip: Because of this right, it is vital that artists own their master to collect royalties from digital audio transmission.

Public Performance in New Technologies

We have discussed live public performance and terrestrial radio. Now it is time to enter a new form of public performance. Public performance includes transmission to the public regardless of "whether the members of the public ... receive it in the same place or in separate places and at the same time or at different times."[126] Accordingly, audio streams are performances because a "stream is an

---

126 17 U.S.C. 101

electronic transmission that renders the musical work audible as it is received by the client-computer's temporary memory. This transmission, like a television or radio broadcast, is a performance because there is a playing of the song that is perceived simultaneously with the transmission."[127] To state a claim for infringement of the performance right, a plaintiff must establish that (1) the public performance or display of the copyrighted work was for profit, and (2) the defendant lacked authorization from the plaintiff or the plaintiff's representative.[128]

As technology creates more ways for songs to be publicly performed, the definition of public performance is updated and expanded. It now states that a song streamed on the Internet is also a public performance of that song. Therefore, if someone wants to stream a song on the Internet, there must be a license in place with the person who wrote it and the sound recording owner per Section 106(6). This is a minefield because the major music publishers and record labels know this is where music is heading, and they want to get the best deal possible. Further, it is complicated because many of these new ways of digesting music do not fall neatly into a public performance or a reproduction (triggering a mechanical royalty). If you stream a song on YouTube, for example, it is certainly a public performance, but also may technically be a reproduction since it is reproduced on someone's server. Europe has gone to a model that make sense: A download is considered 25% performance and 75% mechanical; while streaming is the exact opposite. Of course, in the U.S. it is not nearly that easy.

Under the laws around the world, the songwriter is granted the exclusive right to publicly perform their song. This means that no one else can "publicly" play (either their recording of it or someone else's recording of it) without negotiating a license with the songwriter/publisher to do so. Therefore, if the song is streamed on the Internet via Apple, YouTube, Napster, Rhapsody, Spotify, Myspace, Google, etc., a license must be negotiated with the songwriter/publisher for the public performance of the song. If a license is not negotiated, for the public performance, like BMI, then the songwriter can sue for copyright infringement in theory.

---

127 United States v. Am. Soc. Of Composers, Authors, & Publishers, 627 F.3d 64, 74 (2d Cir.2010).

128 See Broad. Music, Inc. v. 315 W. 44th St. Rest. Corp., No. 93 Civ. 8082(MBM), 1995 WL 408399, at *2 (S.D.N.Y. July 11, 1995).

To make things even more confusing, if the songwriter chooses to become a member of ASCAP or BMI, the two largest U.S.-based Performing Rights Organizations that negotiate public performance licenses on behalf of their members, the digital store must negotiate "one-to-one" with the PRO for this license. Because of the consent decrees I have discussed, if the digital music store, radio station, restaurant, etc. do not like the royalty rate that BMI and/or ASCAP are demanding to publicly perform the songwriter's song, they can turn to the U.S. government to argue their case and the government can rule on the rate.

Unfortunately for the digital stores, the three licenses are split between three (or four) separate entities: The songwriter, the record label for the sound recording of the song, the publisher (if different from the songwriter), for the reproduction (mechanical royalty), and the organization representing the songwriter for the public performance of her song (BMI/ASCAP). There may be a lot of overlap there, and for indie artists, it may be just the artist herself. For a digital store to stream the songwriter's song, it needs to negotiate and get licenses from all the rights holders. The tension and disagreements between the entities representing these rights usually stall or stop negotiations.

The Copyright Rate Board (CRB) is mandated by statute to set rates and typically encourages both music licensors and licensees to negotiate on rate settlements. But, more often than not, a consensus cannot be reached and so a rate trial proceeds, wherein all interested parties make their cases through statements and testimony. After listening to testimony, the judges decide as to what the statutory royalty rates will be for the upcoming five-year period.

A recent New York rate court ruling concluded that a BMI proposed rate of 2.5% of revenue for public performances from Pandora was "reasonable, and indeed at the low end of the range of fees of recent licenses." Given the recent industry deals made in the free market, the court agreed with BMI that this rate is a more appropriate reflection of the value of BMI's music.

Streaming Overview

Streaming is the future of music. More than 80 million users and growing are streaming music. In 2014, streaming audio revenue was $1.87 billion, surpassing CD sales. That's all streaming audio, but most of that is music, and it is growing even more. The increase in streaming has directly led to a decline in album sales. If you understand that, you have a better chance of understanding the law and economics of music. If I can stream an album, I have little incentive to buy it.

The music industry is moving quickly to a streaming model, where people pay a recurring fee (or allow ads if they do not pay) to listen to music on-demand usually via an Internet connection. For example, stores and sites like Rhapsody, MOG, Napster and Spotify provide this type of "on-demand" streaming service. A customer just needs to be connected to the Internet, or, when they are not connected, be pre-approved to listen to what music they want when they want. If you pay, you typically can listen to music "offline."

In 2013, for the first time ever, sales of traditional downloads dropped (buying music from iTunes, Amazon, etc.), while streaming services like Spotify, Vevo, Pandora, and others racked up 118 BILLION streams. This was an increase of 32% according to Nielsen SoundScan. Said Daniel Glass of Glassnote Records (label of Mumford & Sons), "I have never seen an evolution this quick. Streaming income is getting better every period."[129]

Big players are starting to get involved as a result. Microsoft has Xbox music, which is bundled with every Windows. Google and Apple also have new streaming services. Beats Music, founded by Jimmy Iovine and Trent Reznor, has more than $60 million in capital to launch its paid streaming service.[130]

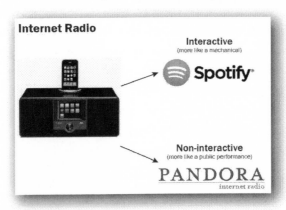

---

129 Rolling Stone Magazine, Aug. 6, 2013.
130 Rolling Stone, Feb. 15, 2014.

Interactive v. Non-Interactive Streaming

There is a distinction between interactive and non-interactive streams. Interactive streaming is when the listener affirmatively plays the song, like when you listen to a song or album on Spotify.[131] Interactive streams are considered **both** a mechanical and a public performance, so artists can get paid both when their song is streamed, though the rates are quite low. Conversely, if you are Spotify, then you need permission from the publishers via the PROs **and** Harry Fox (since it is both), plus, the sound recording copyright holders (likely major labels collected via SoundExchange). Major music publishers and record labels have agreed that there is a 30-second promotional exception for interactive streaming.

A non-interactive stream is one that is played, or programmed for you, like a DJ would. Pandora would be a good example of this. This is considered a "public performance" and the artist gets paid through their PRO and the provider gets a blanket license with the publisher via a PRO. This is **not** considered a mechanical since there is no reproduction, so Harry Fox is not involved. Further, since this a "digital audio transmission," the sound recording holders will get paid, again via SoundExchange. This fee is fixed by law, but it's complicated. Radio stations that are terrestrial, but simulcast on the Internet must pay the sound recording holder via SoundExchange.

Practice Tip: In general, both the song composer and the master recording rights holder get paid for both types of streaming; but, interactive is considered both a mechanical and a performance, while non-interactive is just a performance.

Streams for music services add a whole new complexity to the situation as every single time a song is streamed not only does the record label have to be paid, but so must the person who wrote the song because streams, believe it or not, are reproductions and public performances, in some instances.

---

131 Spotify does have a radio component as well, though it is primarily used where you click on a song or album.

Interactive Streaming Revenue

While streaming is the new model, most artists cannot sustain themselves alone on album sales, which are declining. Streaming has not made up the difference. Consumers are not as inclined to buy an album when they can stream it (and millions of other albums) for free (or a modest monthly fee). That's why some artists like Taylor Swift and The Black Keys have pulled most of their music off Spotify. Others like Lucinda Williams have all their music on there, but not their most recent releases.[132]

Song downloads from iTunes have dropped 39% in five years, but streaming revenue is not making up for the loss in sales for musicians. Streaming revenue requires massive numbers to see significant income. Previously, if an artist had 10,000 albums sold on iTunes, they could rely on $70,000 ($10 for album sale less iTunes' 30% cut) in sales when a new album was released. This does not even count album sales on the road, where they would keep all the revenue, less the costs of reproduction. However, now, even if each fan listens to a 10-song album on Spotify 10 times in the first few months (1,000,000 plays), that would only net about $5,000 (and much less if those plays were on YouTube). Even if there were 50,000 additional listeners to the album only twice, that's just an additional $5,000.

Interactive sites like Spotify are required to pay the songwriter a mechanical royalty, which is a combination of a percentage of the revenue generated by the site and a payment per each subscriber. So far, it is not a bonanza for artists. Bands earn .004 cent per stream and do not make much (labels seem to be making the dough though). For example, the band Galaxie 500's song "Tugboat" streamed 7,800 times on Pandora and the band's three songwriters got a combined 21 cents.[133]

This is a true hybrid of both a mechanical and public performance. The streaming services pay a percentage of either subscription fees or ad revenue. Sometimes it is a payment from 15 to 50 cents per subscriber per month. The percentages vary anywhere from 10% to 22% of gross revenue or subscription fees, which includes more than 5% that goes to the PROs (the rest going

---

132 Lucinda does not have her two most recent albums on Spotify.
133 Rolling Stone, Dec. 6, 2012.

for mechanicals). So, the PROs get their share (divided by their secret formula), and the rest goes to the publishers on the mechanical and performance side of things. This is simplified, so for a full explanation, go to the federal regulations.[134]

The following is from HFA's Songfile rates for interactive streaming, but these numbers need to be confirmed because I think they seem too high and conflict with other numbers I've seen for streaming rates for songwriters that are much lower.

Rates for interactive streaming in limited quantities of between 100 and 10,000 streams:

The royalty rate for interactive streams through Songfile is $0.01 per stream.
For example, the royalty rate for 500 interactive streams is $5.00.
The royalty rate for 5,000 interactive streams is $50.00.

For quantities more than 10,000 streams, licenses for interactive streaming can be obtained through our bulk licensing process. If you are interested in obtaining such licenses, please contact newmedia@harryfox.com. Please note that to satisfy your obligations pursuant to the bulk licensing process for the distribution of interactive streams, you must be able to report information such as service revenue, subscriber information, content costs, and applicable performance royalty expenses. Compare the above from Harry Fox to what I have found online, and this is for both the mechanical and public performance.

Comparison of Streaming Sites -- What They Pay Artists

Slacker: Pays .0012 cent/stream ($1.20 for 1000 streams); Artist gets 70 cents of .99 song sold

iTunes Radio: Pays .0013 cent/stream, but this is only suggested—not been implemented yet ($1.30 for 1000 streams); Artist gets 70 of 99 cents song sold

---

134 37 CFR, part 385.

Spotify: Pays .001-.005 cent/stream ($1-$5 for 1000 streams)

Deezer: Pays .0081 cent/stream ($8.10 for 1000 streams)

Rdio: Less than .01 cent/stream, and will also pay for how many subscribers an artist has, including $10 for each referred fan (less than $10 for 1000 streams)

Pandora: .0012 cent/stream ($1.20 for 1000 streams)

Apple has filed a new proposal with the U.S. Copyright Royalty Board which it hopes will simplify songwriting royalties in the States.

CDs through Amazon: Artist gets 69 out of 99 cents.

This puts the industry average at $.00217 per stream. To make $1 an artist's song would have to be streamed 461 times! Here's a great story about a band's way around these low streaming rates. A band called Vulfpeck had a "Sleepify" album. They put up a silent album of 30-second songs and encouraged their fans to put it on repeat at night while they slept. They made $20,000 before Spotify took it down claiming it was against their terms of service.

It should be noted that some sites pay better than others. For example, sites like Jay Z's Tidal pay artists more because you must pay to listen (and the business was started by artists). Artists are now beginning to exclusively release (at least for a period of time) their work on streaming sites. Beyonce's "Lemonade" is only available on Tidal. Apple's new streaming site has been particularly active in this area. Artists as diverse as Radiohead, Chance the Rapper and Drake have released albums exclusively on streaming sites. Perhaps this value add will bump up paying customers for these services. The Cupertino giant has suggested that all on-demand streaming services should pay songwriters a statutory rate of 9.1 cents every 100 plays. That's a per-stream rate of $0.00091, and works out to $910 per million streams, or $910,000 for a billion.

Spotify pays about 10% of its revenue to songwriters (split between mechanical and performance royalties) and about 60% to the artists. Services like Spotify do not have to negotiate with songwriters, because the government sets the rates, through the consent decree for PROs and a compulsory license for mechanical licenses. Mechanical royalties for songwriting are usually paid by labels or artists to a third party. Traditionally, for the major publishers it has been HFA (the Harry Fox Agency) who pays the publishers.

Only the artists getting millions of plays are seeing significant, livable income solely from streaming. And most of them are with labels who take the majority (or all) of that income. Plus, they are likely established artists who do not need the revenue as much anyway because they can get it through touring, merchandise, or album sales.

Streaming Revenue: Non-Interactive Streaming and Satellite Radio

This is a performance since it is like radio, but not over-the-air terrestrial radio. Publishers usually get a percentage of revenue, with minimums, but certainly work out deals with big players such as Pandora. They would also pay the sound recording holder as well. This is not considered a mechanical royalty.

Digital performances like Pandora pay a recording digital performance royalty to SoundExchange and a songwriting digital performance royalty to the PROs. But on the flipside, BMI and ASCAP are governed by consent decrees, which means an arm of the U.S. Judicial Branch (called a "ratecourt" --did we already define this above?) can set the rates (per radio play, per stream, etc.). BMI and ASCAP collect for songwriting performance royalties. In exchange for the right to collect on behalf of songwriters across America, they are limited in their ability to negotiate by this rate court.

SoundExchange is not governed by a consent decree, which means they can negotiate on the free market. This is where things get complicated. Recording artists get paid nothing when their music is played on AM/FM radio (because there's no performance right for recordings on terrestrial radio), but they are typically paid at least five times more than songwriters when music is performed digitally, like on Pandora. That's because of SoundExchange's negotiation power (backed by the three major labels), and BMI/ASCAP's limitations. AM/FM broadcasters do pay songwriters, but it is at a royalty rate ultimately set by the courts. There will be more on SoundExchange in the next chapter.

Spotify Sued: Mechanicals v. Masters

The disparity that I referred to above in payments between the sound recording and the composition may explain why Spotify has been sued. On December

28, 2015, David Lowery, who runs the Trichordist blog and fronts the bands Camper Van Beethoven and Cracker, filed a class-action lawsuit seeking at least $150 million in damages against Spotify. The lawsuit alleges that Spotify knowingly, willingly and unlawfully reproduces and distributes compositions without obtaining mechanical licenses.

The lawsuit alleges that not only does Spotify not pay the mechanicals to publishers, but also fails to get permission from the publisher (the compulsory license). Streaming services, however, do not have to get permission to use a composition, but they do have to obtain a license for it. A license can either be obtained directly from the publisher or they can send a Notice of Intent (NOI) to the publisher just saying that they intend to use the composition (30 days prior to releasing the song on the service). If you sign up with a third party publisher, presumably they would give Spotify permission, but there are lots of songwriters that are independent.

The Importance of a Third Party Publisher

In addition to digital distribution, companies like CD Baby and TuneCore also offer publishing for indie musicians. Given the complexity of this area, not to mention the impossibility of indie and/or DIY artists possibly tracking all these royalties, it is more vital now more than ever to have a professional handle this.

Practice Tip: Hire a third party collect all your publishing income (mechanicals, public performance, licensing), including international royalties.

If you have a third party publisher, you do not need to register with Harry Fox or a PRO to collect mechanical royalties because they will collect mechanical royalties for you. Further, you cannot register with HFA[135]

---

135 HFA was recently bought by SESAC, perhaps indicating that SESAC wants to diversify and get in on mechanicals in addition to public performance royalties.

unless you are a publisher and have songs released by a third party label and not self-released.

An iTunes download in the U.S. nets you $.69 (70% of $.99 - Apple retains 30% from iTunes sales) whereas a download in England nets you around $.60. So, if you do not have an admin publishing company, you will not get any of your international mechanical royalties from download sales. These international collections agencies will hold onto this money for about three years until a publisher comes to claim it. You technically could try to do this by calling up collections agencies in every country, but I just recommend going with an admin publishing company because no one has the time or inclination to collect all that.

Spotify, for example, already pays mechanical royalties directly to HFA, and then HFA pays publishers. Rdio already pays mechanical royalties directly to Music Reports Inc., and MRI pays publishers. And international collections agencies grab mechanical royalties from international streaming services like Deezer and pay publishers directly. Loudr, Songfile and Easy Song Licensing ask you how many interactive streams you anticipate, but this is ONLY for SoundCloud, Bandcamp or hosting a streaming player on your website (via Bandzoogle or something like that).

Covers

If you cover a song, the songwriter-publisher would collect all the streaming revenue noted above. You also need to obtain the compulsory license. However, there is no obligation to get a license for a cover from a self-streaming site, like SoundCloud, that is not being monetized, so this area falls through the cracks. Further, it is unlikely a publisher is going to sue you for hosting a streaming cover song on your website. For one, it would be nearly impossible to audit, and, even if for some reason you were getting millions of streams on SoundCloud, the rate you'd owe would not be $.01 per stream, but rather the compulsory streaming rate set by the government which deals with an extremely complicated formula which is based off the streaming services subscriber number and total revenue.

Conclusion

You do not need a mechanical license for the following:

* reproduction of sound recordings;
* putting a song in a video;
* performing the song in public;
* displaying or reprinting lyrics;
* using the song in digital jukeboxes, ringbacks, or background music;
* printing sheet music;
* using the song in karaoke.

You would, however, need the publisher's permission for all the above except sound recording reproduction and playing it live in public.

Sources of revenue for artists and how it is calculated:

1. Radio: Logs and digital monitoring services
2. Television: Cue sheets and digital monitoring
3. Digital Radio: Provider records
4. Live Events: Venue set lists
5. Muzak

The PROs collect royalties from TV and radio. SoundExchange collects royalties from Internet broadcasters for use of the master recordings. As a practical matter, songwriters just collect royalties via blanket licenses each time their song is play in a "public performance." The third party would save you from registering your works globally with performing and mechanical rights societies, and potentially sound recording collection agencies. A Publishing Administrator plays the role of a kind of "distributor" to the global performing rights and mechanical societies to make sure your compositions are properly registered and collecting royalties wherever they are being performed or sold.

To summarize, these third parties would collect:

*   publishing revenue from synchronization rights of music to film/TV, video games, or commercial. (collected by publisher);
*   publishing revenue from lyric print rights used in music apps, books and magazines, apparel, websites (like the lyric websites), or sheet music, such as MusicNotes.com. (collected by publisher);
*   publishing revenue from compulsory mechanical licenses for record labels or indie artists to record and distribute music works (such as doing a song placed with a major artist or an indie artist doing a cover of a song previously performed by a major artist) whether posted on YouTube or sold on a CD. (collected by Harry Fox Agency);
*   publishing revenue from DART royalties from Audio Home Recording Act of 1992 distributed to the Music Publishers Subfund and Writers Subfund (collected by Copyright Office);136
*   publishing revenue from public performance via ASCAP, BMI, or SESAC (Note: A songwriter can only be registered to one of these guys);
*   publishing revenue from foreign monies via sub-publishing agreements and other licensing arrangements in foreign territories. (collected by PROs, publishers and other collecting entities depending on the nature of the royalties and legislation);
*   publishing revenue from hundreds of other licensing sources (collected by PROs, publishers and other collecting entities depending on the nature of the royalties and territory).

I will say this again. If you are an artist, do everything you can to control your own publishing and own as much of it as you can.

---

136 See 17 U.S.C. 1001 et. seq. DART royalties consist of payments made to the U.S. Copyright Office for "blank CDs and personal audio devices, media centers, satellite radio dishes, and car audio systems that have recording capabilities."

Chapter 20

● ● ●

SOUNDEXCHANGE

I have discussed them before, but SoundExchange (SoundExchange.com) is a service (like PROs) that collects revenue for the master rights holders of the sound recording when their work is played via digital audio transmission, such as streaming. This can be record labels or the band/songwriter. So, if your Taylor Swift cover blows up, SoundExchange will pay you royalties on the sound recording, and Taylor's PRO will pay her royalties on the public performance. SoundExchange was created by the major record labels, who own most of the valuable sound recordings.

To monitor and collect sound recording money, the music streaming companies provide detailed electronic play logs which are matched to individual recordings allowing SoundExchange to pay out exactly what is earned for sound recordings. As soon as you sign up online for free with SoundExchange, you can collect royalties you have earned dating back as far as three years ago for your sound recordings. As of October 2016, I was told by SoundExchange that they can go back to January 1, 2012. If you earned sound recording revenue prior to that, then you lose it.

According to SoundExchange.com, digital royalties are fees that digital radio services, such as Pandora, SiriusXM, webcasters and cable TV music channels are required by law to pay for streaming music. These royalties are paid by the services to SoundExchange, via playlists of all the recordings played by the service provider.

SoundExchange takes these payments, allocates the fees to the recordings according to how often each song was played, and then pays the featured artist(s) and/or copyright owners of those recordings. More than 90,000 artists and 28,000 sound recording copyright owners have registered with SoundExchange, and they have paid out nearly $2 billion in royalties since their first distribution.

Under the law, 45 percent of performance royalties are paid directly to the featured artists on a recording, and 5 percent are paid to a fund for non-featured artists, typically session musicians and background singers. The other 50 percent of the performance royalties are paid to the owner of the sound recording (i.e. the owner of the "master"), which can be a record label or an artist who owns their own masters. If you are both the featured artist and copyright owner (a singer/songwriter like myself) you would get both (95%).

The term "featured artist" refers to the group or individual most prominently featured on the sound recording. If you have questions about who qualifies as a featured artist, or wish to register as a featured artist on a recording, contact SoundExchange's customer service department.

Spotify, iTunes Radio, and Rdio have struck deals with labels and distributors to pay digital performance royalties directly to rights holders, thus bypassing SoundExchange. But again, digital performance royalties are only owed for non-interactive streams which occur within those services' radio-like features, **not** in their on-demand capacities.

There are lots of other sound recording royalties (besides the digital royalties collected by SoundExchange) that are collected on behalf of featured recording artists, non-featured artists (e.g. background or session vocalists), instrumental musicians, etc. They include:

* sound recording revenue (also known as DART royalties, which stands for Digital Audio Recorders and Tapes) generated from the U.S. Audio Home Recording Act of 1992 (AHRA). Manufacturers and importers of audio home recording devices (such as tape recorders) and audio home recording media (such as blank CDs) pay a royalty to the Copyright Office;

* sound recording revenue generated from reciprocal Private Copy agreements with numerous foreign collectives in countries that also have legislation providing these royalties such as: Japan, the Netherlands, Hungary, Spain, Portugal, Greece, Germany, Latvia, and Estonia, just to name a few;
* sound recording revenue from record rentals remuneration from Japan, where sound recordings are rented in much the same manner DVDs are rented here in the U.S.;
* sound recording revenue generated from digital public performance from the Digital Performance Right in Sound Recordings Act of 1995 (DPRA) and the Digital Millennium Copyright Act (DMCA) paid to SoundExchange (as discussed above);
* sound recording revenue generated from a treaty with AIE, Sociedad de Gestión – the Spanish Rights Collective. The Audiovisual Division of the AFM & SAG-AFTRA Intellectual Property Rights Distribution Fund (established in 2010) distributes payments collected from any television show or motion picture that is broadcast on Spanish television and contains the performance of an AFM or SAG-AFTRA vocalist;
* sound recording revenue collected by the Symphonic Royalties division of the AFM & SAG-AFTRA Intellectual Property Rights Distribution Fund, which are royalties for performers on symphonic sound recordings, including musicians and singers of an orchestra.
* sound recording revenue from master use licenses between record companies and film/TV production companies (TV shows, movies, and web series), advertisers (commercials and products), video games; and
* sound recording revenue from compulsory mechanical licenses for sample use in other songs, copies and re-distribution, and ringtones.

Now, sites like Pandora, pay both digital sound recording performance royalties (to SoundExchange), and digital composition performance royalties (to PROs). There is a Consent Decree that gave about 10x more for sound recording royalties (to SoundExchange) than for songwriter royalties (to the PROs).

The Songwriter Equity Act has been in Congress for about two years now to make this more equitable.

SoundExchange will hold your back royalties for at least three years, so register now if you have not already. And if you have registered a while ago, make sure you have also registered as the Sound Recording Copyright Owner (previously called the "Rights Owner"). Because the "Both" option is very new, you may have missed it and are only receiving 45% of your total money and not 95%.

If you are a session musician AND in the AFM (musician's union), 5% of the total money earned for each song has been reserved for you. Contact the AFM to join and be entitled to this money. Here's SoundExchange's breakdown for payment:

45% to Featured Artist
50% to the Sound Recording Owner (label - or you if self-released)
5% to session musicians, e.g. "non-featured artists."[137]

Regardless if you have session musicians or not on your record, SoundExchange holds 5% of all royalties from everyone for them; thus, you can only get 95%.

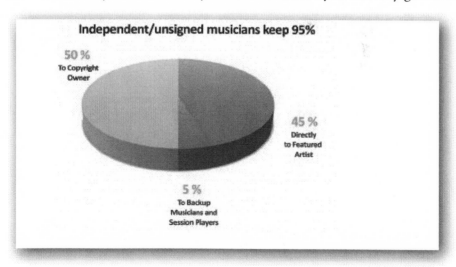

---

137 You must be a member of the musician's union SAG-AFTRA.

Practice Tip: Composers in a band earn publishing that non-composers will not earn, but a band can certainly share in the sound recording royalties. If you are a solo artist, you may likely be both. The main thing is for an indie band to register your songs via SoundExchange to collect this revenue, or make sure your publisher is collecting it. If you are on a major, your label is likely keeping all, or most, of this revenue.

Below are two screenshots that bands or artists must fill out on SoundExchange.

Who are you registering?

SoundExchange pays royalties to both the featured artist(s) on a sound recording, and the copyright owner of the recording.

Yourself Are you registering on your own behalf? Register yourself as a Featured Artist performer, a Sound Recording Copyright Owner, or both.

Someone Else Are you registering on behalf of someone else or a group of individuals who receive payment as a collective entity (which they wholly own)? You will be required to submit a signed SoundExchange Authorization form for each performer you are registering today.

What are you registering as?

Performer   Sound Recording Copyright Owner   Both

☐ I hereby certify that I am at least 18 years of age.   Save & Continue

Do you record as a solo artist?

If yes, list each solo name you record under (enter one at a time, please). If no, then leave blank and proceed to the next question on this screen.

Add

Solo Artist Name

Do you record as a member of any bands?

If yes, provide each band name that you have recorded with as a featured artist member of the band (enter one at a time, please).

Band Name

%   Does that apply to all recordings by this band?   Add

What percentage of royalties do you claim? ⓘ   ○ Yes ○ No

Back   Save & Continue

Chapter 21

● ● ●

YOUTUBE AND THE DIGITAL MILLENNIUM COPYRIGHT ACT

YouTube is a website that not only features music videos, but also streams music and even whole albums. It is where musicians are discovered. Also, it pays a mechanical royalty that is computed as a percentage of ad sales if you are on a major label. A band can certainly upload their videos to YouTube, but you can also do so for just your songs; maybe they have lyrics scrolling or just a picture of your album cover. If you have a third party as publisher, they will get your music on YouTube.

Practice Tip: YouTube is not just for videos anymore. In fact, it has only been recently eclipsed by streaming in the amount of listening.

YouTube is also where a lot of covers are done. In April 2013, the Universal Music Publishing Group reached a new agreement with YouTube which will allow its English-speaking repertoire to be played (covered) on the social media website in 127 countries in Europe, the Middle East, Africa and Asia. The deal encompasses all types of YouTube videos that feature music, including user-generated content of covers of songs in Universal's catalog.

So, songwriters, Universal wants you to cover their songs and they have quite a catalog. In general, keep in mind that technically if you cover a song and put an image with it, you are making a new work (music video) and need the publisher's permission. This certainly does not get followed much on YouTube, (or most songwriters do not care if you put up a video of some-one's child dancing to their song), but I want you to know what the law is. It is the same as having to get a sync license for a commercial, movie, or TV show.

Vevo is a catalog on YouTube that contains videos from the major labels. Vevo is a bedrock for music videos on the Internet. It offers 200,000 official music videos that draw 18 billion views a month globally on its popular YouTube channel and its own site and app. Yet most would struggle to recall its name.

Collecting YouTube Royalties

Audiam is a company that gets artists paid when their music is used on YouTube and other places like Spotify. Companies like TuneCore and CD Baby also do the same. There is no compulsory license with video streaming, so the CRB has no jurisdiction in this area. Thus, publishers can get whatever they can from YouTube or Vevo without the threat that those entities would go to the CRB and get a lower rate.

Major Label world: The majors have cut deals with the players that cover both the video and the publishing rights. The labels get a whopping 70% of ad revenues and/or subscription monies. This includes the publisher's share, assuming the labels are not the publisher. So, the publisher and label have their own deal on how revenue is to be split, typically the publisher would get 10-15%.

User-generated content (UGC) and the DIY label world: Since the majors are not involved, YouTube, in theory, would have to go through all the individual songwriters/publishers, or through Harry Fox. So, Fox and YouTube came to a deal which is available to anyone who wants it. UGC that has a commercial version of the song gets 15% of net ad revenues. If it is a new recording, the publisher gets anywhere from 35-50% of net ad revenues, depending upon whether the user has his/her own channel and gets some of that revenue. Go to YouTubelicenseoffer.com for the full deal. All of this can be quite confusing and the numbers make calculus seem quaint, and I am someone who follows this stuff.

Practice Tip: The easiest solution for independent artists is to sign up with a digital distribution company and let then collect these monies on your behalf for a small fee or percentage. They even do sync licensing and YouTube revenue. The money is not enough for you to chase it down via your own music publishing company. Major artists have major publishers or enough clout and resources to have their own publishing company to handle this aspect; plus, they likely have a catalog that generates enough income to make it worthwhile.

Here's a paragraph from TuneCore regarding YouTube:

> When a subscriber streams your music, you get paid a proportionate share of YouTube Music Key's subscription revenue per month calculated on terms set out in TuneCore's blanket agreement with the store (this usually excludes streams during a subscriber's free trial). Payments will fluctuate each month, depending on the amount of subscription revenue generated and how often your music was streamed.

Your songs generate money on YouTube when your music is used in other people's videos and on your own YouTube videos.

The following is from CD Baby:

So, how does monetizing music on YouTube work?
YouTube's content ID system

Once you've opted in for CD Baby's Sync Licensing Program, your music will be delivered to YouTube's content ID system. This means that YouTube will scan your tracks with their magical high-tech machinery and register an exact sonic "fingerprint" for each one of your songs in their database.

From that point on, anytime someone out there in the YouTube universe uploads a video which uses one of your songs, YouTube will place an ad on that video and you will earn a share of any ad revenue generated.

Remember, this includes placing ads on the videos you have already uploaded to your own YouTube channel — but more on that later!

When will I earn ad revenue from YouTube? And how much money will I make?

If a video on YouTube features your music, YouTube will serve up an ad. That video will generate ad revenue if the text or banner ad is clicked — or, if it's a commercial that is a pre-roll before your video, you'll earn a share of ad revenue if the viewer watches the entire ad (if shorter than 30 seconds) or a minimum of 30 seconds of the ad (for commercials longer than 30 seconds).

There's no real way to estimate how much you'll make from ad revenue on YouTube, because the ad rates vary depending on many factors. YouTube is a Google company, after all, and YouTube ad placements are bid upon by advertisers. Plus, advertisers pay a different amount depending on the type of ad that's run, the popularity of the video/channel/network, etc.

So, while it's difficult to give an average payout per ad or per artist, you WILL be able to view a complete breakdown of your YouTube ad revenue in your CD Baby members account. The more videos on YouTube using your music, the more money you can make.

Once YouTube has fingerprinted your music in their content ID process, every video that contains your music will can generate ad revenue for you — so the more the merrier. Encourage your friends, fans, and family to use your music in their crazy cat videos and holiday party blooper reels.

What happens to the videos I've uploaded myself? And why am I seeing a notice saying that I don't control the rights to my video on YouTube?

YouTube is a brilliant invention, but it's only a machine. It doesn't actually "know" your music or know that YOU created those lovely tunes. So it's going to place ads on the videos in your channel too (if they feature your music).

In the eyes of YouTube, your songs are all just nameless, faceless digital files with meta tags letting them know that CD Baby administers the rights, and they're going to pay ad revenue for those usages to CD Baby (since you've elected for us to administer your licensing rights in this circumstance). Simple: YouTube pays the third party, and they pay you the musician.

It's important to remember, we're only claiming the administrative right to license your music and collect money on your behalf. You retain 100% ownership of your music and can cancel your involvement in CD Baby's Sync Licensing Program at any time. Long story short, if you log into your YouTube account and see a notice that says "matched third party content"– don't worry!

YouTube: Matched Third Party Content

As I mentioned above, no one is claiming ownership of your music. This just means that YouTube's content ID system identified your song correctly and registered that CD Baby is the party you've authorized to collect ad revenue on your behalf.

What should I do if YouTube shows me a "matched third party content" notice concerning videos I've uploaded that contain my own music? If you see this warning, it's an indicator that your music is now ready for monetization on YouTube. Simply click on the "Matched third party content" link. It will take you to a page that looks like this:

YouTube: Matched Third Party Content
If you would like CD Baby to continue monetizing your music on YouTube, click "Acknowledge."

Then what? You go make some more music and let CD Baby collect money from YouTube for you. And hey, since you saw the "third party matched content" notice for your videos, you'll have the peace of mind that the system is working just as it should for all videos featuring your music.

I'm already a YouTube partner and have ad revenue set up for the videos in my channel, will the exclusive content ID rights affect my standing with the revenue stream on my videos?

This will not interfere with your monetized videos that DO NOT contain music that is a part of the CD Baby Sync program. But it's possible that it could interfere with your videos that do contain music you've opted-in for CD Baby's Sync Licensing Program.

If you are already making money from monetizing your YouTube channel, CD Baby will still collect revenue for the videos that contain your songs that are a part of our YouTube monetization program.

In that event, you can do one of the following things:

* Keep things simple and let us [CD Baby] take over the management of ad revenues for your YouTube channel. There are no payout thresholds to meet when you go through CD Baby.
* Have CD Baby "whitelist" your channel. This will allow you to continue collect revenues directly from your channel while giving CD Baby the ability to collect ad revenue whenever your music appears in someone else's video.
* Opt-out of CD Baby's YouTube monetization program. However, this will remove your music from YouTube's Content ID system that enables you to make money off other videos on YouTube that are using your music.

Digital Millennium Copyright Act

Congress passed The Digital Millennium Copyright Act (DMCA) to address issues with respect to the "First Sale Doctrine" in the digital age. It states that while you may purchase a digital copy of a song, you do not have the right to then distribute it digitally in the same way you can resell a CD to a used CD store. The rationale, of course, relates to exclusive rights of the copyright holder to reproduce and distribute their work. When you resell or lend a physical CD that you have bought, you are handing over (distributing) the very same copy of the work that you bought. You are not reproducing that copy. On the other hand, under the law, you are not allowed to buy a CD, burn a copy of it, and sell that burned copy to a used CD store, because you are violating the exclusive right to reproduce.

Similarly, in a digital world, you cannot download a song to your hard drive, and then sell a copy of that song (keeping a copy on your hard drive), because you are reproducing and distributing the work, and you do not have the right to do so. It should be noted that if someone violates the right of reproduction they will almost certainly violate the right of distribution. I discussed this in the distribution section.

Much of the DMCA deals with illegal UGC on the web, particularly YouTube. Under the DMCA, if you feel your copyright has been infringed, you can send notice to the infringer's Copyright Agent containing the following information in accordance with the Digital Millennium Copyright Act: (i) a physical or electronic signature of the copyright owner or a person authorized to act on their behalf; (ii) identification of the copyrighted work claimed to have been infringed; (iii) identification of the material that is claimed to be infringing or to be the subject of infringing activity and that is to be removed or access to which is to be disabled, and information reasonably sufficient to permit us to locate the material; (iv) your contact information, including your address, telephone number, and an email address; (v) a statement by you that you have a good faith belief that use of the material in the manner complained of is not authorized by the copyright owner, its agent, or the law; and (vi) a statement that the information in the notification is accurate, and, under penalty of perjury, that you are authorized to act on behalf of the copyright owner.[138]

The main flaw under the DMCA concerns websites like Grooveshark and YouTube because they have users upload material, they can claim ignorance, and just take the offending material down when they get a take-down letter and after many have already seen or listened to it. This is why YouTube has been sued by a number of media giants such as Viacom, who complain that whole episodes of shows such as "The Daily Show" appear in whole on

---

138 See 17 U.S.C. 512.

YouTube, and, by the time they are taken down, millions may have already seen it and the network is out advertising revenue.

Some artists do not care whether others post their music without permission, and others do. That is your call depending on where your career is at and your perspective that any publicity is good and everyone owns the music, or being very protective of your songs. I will say this though: You cannot stop all copyright infringement so do not worry about it—it's like speeding—everyone does it to some extent; just catch the ones who go really fast!

If you upload music or a music video to YouTube, make sure you have the rights to do so. Here's a Copyright Checklist from SoundCloud for those uploading music on their website:

Can you answer "yes" to all the following questions?

* Did you compose the music yourself?
* Did you write the lyrics yourself?
* Did you record and produce the track yourself or do you have permission from the producer or record label that made the recording?
* Do you have written permission from all copyright owners to use any samples contained in the track?

Does a Mechanical License Apply to YouTube?

It is complicated. This is a hybrid between a public performance and a mechanical. Either way, the publisher gets paid. Once you sync any video or image with a song, you need a "synchronization license." You are warranting that you have cleared all necessary rights to the video when you upload or publish it to YouTube. Under YouTube's Help section, it explains its policy on copyright infringement: "YouTube respects the rights of copyright holders and publishers and requires all users to confirm they own the copyright or have permission from the copyright holder to upload content. We comply with the Digital Millennium Copyright Act (DMCA) and other applicable copyright laws and promptly remove content when properly notified. Repeat infringers' videos are removed and their accounts are terminated and permanently blocked from using YouTube."

Some major labels have negotiated deals with YouTube to monetize cover versions of songs they control through their publishing arms. You should still get the sync license, but these labels may look the other way in order to make money off your cover.

In Capital Records v. Vimeo,[139] the Second Circuit concluded that the safe harbor must include pre-1972 recordings, or the entire "compromise" envisaged by Congress would be illusory. What Congress intended in passing Section 512(c) was to strike a compromise under which, in return for the obligation to take down infringing works promptly on receipt of notice of infringement from the owner, Internet service providers would be relieved of liability for user-posted infringements of which they were unaware, as well as of the obligation to scour matter posted on their services to ensure against copyright infringement. The purpose of the compromise was to make economically feasible the provision of valuable Internet services while expanding protections of the interests of copyright owners through the new notice-and-takedown provision. To construe Section 512(c) as leaving service providers subject to liability under state copyright laws for postings by users of infringements of which the service providers were unaware would defeat the very purpose Congress sought to achieve in passing the statute.

DMCA and Streaming

In June 2016, a group of prominent artists such as Paul McCartney and Taylor Swift, led by former Eagles manager Irving Azoff, signed a petition urging Congress to reform the Digital Millennium Copyright Act. The artists contend that the Act, which was written in 1998, is outdated. Their main complaint is the lack of money paid to them, and their main protagonist seems to be YouTube. While streaming rates need to be higher for all artists, these huge musicians may be the wrong messenger targeting the wrong problem. The DMCA mainly deals with providing Internet service providers (ISP's) a "safe

---

139 2016 U.S. App. LEXIS 10884.

harbor" to take down infringing material after receiving notice of such. These artists seem to link this safe harbor with their lost profits.

Sites such as Spotify (interactive streaming) and YouTube negotiate deals with the major labels and publishers regarding payments. So, these artists, or their respective labels, need to negotiate better deals or threaten to remove their music from YouTube and these other sites.

The Copyright Rate Board (CRB) recently set webcasting rates for sites like Pandora (non-interactive streaming) for the years 2016-2020. It should be noted that this only applies to sound recording royalties, not publishing ones.

Bootlegging Live Performances

In 1994, Congress enacted 17 U.S.C. 1101 to "forbid fixing the sounds or sounds and images of a live musical performance in a copy or phonorecord," without consent of the performers involved. That prohibition extends equally to unauthorized reproduction of "copies or phonorecords of such a performance from an unauthorized fixation."[140] It further holds liable anyone who "distributes or offers to distribute, sells or offers to sell, rents or offers to rent, or traffics in any copy or phonorecord" of the type just described wherever the fixation took place, either in the U.S. or abroad.[141] Further, the statute also forbids transmission or other communication to the public of "the sounds or sounds and images of a live musical performance." This provision creates liability even absent any fixation whatsoever.

Chapter 11 of Title 17 provides that anyone who violates the rights in that section "shall be subject to the remedies provided in sections 502 through 505, to the same extent as an infringer of copyright."[142] Under this language, most civil remedies of copyright law are available against infringers of unfixed musical performances. Unfortunately, Congress failed to incorporate the statute of limitations provision of the Copyright Act, so, in theory, these suits have no statute of limitations. But, while bootlegging is distinct from copyright

---

140 17 U.S.C. 1101(a)(1).
141 17 U.S.C. 1101(b).
142 17 U.S.C. 1101(a)(3).

infringement, the three-year statute of limitations, after all, applies to any "civil action [which] shall be maintained under the provisions of this title," in which the later-added Chapter 11 appears.[143]

---

143 17 U.S.C. 507(b).

Chapter 22

●   ●   ●

FILE SHARING CASES

The advent of digital files not only changed the industry as noted above, it also made it easier to download music illegally. The most common way is what is called peer-to-peer P2P file sharing. This is where a company does not offer songs to download, it facilitates two computers in sharing music. The record industry saw this as illegally reproducing and distributing their sound recordings.

There was very little litigation over violating the distribution right when all music was physical; the focus was more on the reproduction violation. But the advent of Napster in 1999 brought the scope of the distribution right to center stage as copyright owners began to pursue enterprises operating file-sharing networks and those using these networks.

When the Napster file sharing cases came along, courts began relying on Harper & Row, where the US Supreme Court equated publication with distribution. In re Napster, Inc. Copyright Litigation,[144] the court noted the definition of publication under Section 101 "requires either "the distribution of copies or phonorecords of a work to the public by sale or other transfer of ownership, or by rental, lease, or lending," or alternatively, "[t]he offering to distribute copies or phonorecords to a group of persons for purposes of further distribution, public performance, or public display."

---

144 377 F. Supp. 2d 796, 802–805 (N.D.Cal. 2005).

Whereas the first clause plainly requires actual distribution, the second clause contemplates merely an offer of distribution (albeit for "further distribution"). Based on these sources, the court concluded that a "copyright owner seeking to establish that his or her copyrighted work was distributed in violation of section 106(3) must prove that the accused infringer either (1) actually disseminated one or more copies of the work to members of the public or (2) offered to distribute copies of that work for purposes of further distribution, public performance, or public display."[145]

Napster's technology held the indexed files (copyrighted songs and sound recordings) on their central server. So, when Congress amended the law to add safe harbor provisions, Napster was so inundated with takedown requests that it went under. Thus, when other companies started up, they just facilitated the copying via peer-to-peer file sharing to avoid being culpable.

Because of some court decisions that held some file-sharing websites immune from liability because they were technically not making the music "available" to their customers, beginning in 2003, record companies filed lawsuits against thousands of individuals who forensic investigators determined to be active in offering copyrighted works to others. The suits targeted those making files available rather than downloaders. The overwhelming majority of those cases settled, but several alleged file-sharers denied liability. As to those few, their cases proceeded to active litigation.

In sum, the courts have been divided. Some decisions have upheld a violation of the distribution right through offering items to the public. Others have denied that proposition. Still others have followed a middle ground, avoiding the need to choose between the two schools.[146]

In London-Sire Records v. Doe,[147] the court concluded that electronic files constitute material objects. It rejected the notion that the Copyright Act

---

145 377 F. Supp. 2d at 805.

146 See Arista Records LLC v. Does 1-19, 551 F. Supp. 2d 1, 10 (D.D.C. 2008; Arista Records LLC v. Does 1-27, 584 F. Supp. 2d 240, 249 (D. Me. 2008); Maverick Recording Co. v. Harper, 598 F.3d 193, 197 (5th Cir.), cert. denied, 131 S. Ct. 590, 178 L. Ed.2d 511 (2010) (Alito, J., dissenting). Arista Records LLC v. Doe 3, 604 F.3d 110, 122 (2d Cir. 2010) (complaint adequately alleged "that defendants both actually downloaded plaintiffs' copyrighted works and distributed them").

147 542 F. Supp. 2d 153 (D. Mass. 2008).

intends "materiality in its most obvious sense to mean a tangible object with a certain heft, like a book or compact disc."[148] Instead, the opinion reasonably concluded that any object in which a sound recording can be fixed is a "material object." That includes the electronic files at issue here. When a user on a peer-to-peer network downloads a song from another user, he receives into his computer a digital sequence representing the sound recording. That sequence is magnetically encoded on a segment of his hard disk (or likewise written on another media.) With the right hardware and software, the downloader can use the magnetic sequence to reproduce the sound recording. The electronic file (or, perhaps more accurately, the appropriate segment of the hard disk) is therefore a "phonorecord" within the meaning of the statute.[149]

The legislative history of the 1976 Act confirms the proposition that there is no need to show consummated acts of actual distribution. Instead, the intent of Congress was to incorporate a "make available" right into the copyright owner's arsenal.

Congress defined offers to distribute to constitute "publication" and then, on the face of the statute, used the phrase "exclusive right of publication" interchangeably with "the exclusive right to distribute." It even classified importation as constituting "an infringement of the exclusive right to distribute copies or phonorecords under section 106," without any need to show that the infringed item was distributed to any third party.

Conclusion

Revisiting the ReDigi case, which held that selling "used" MP3's did not fall under the First Sale Doctrine, the court noted that with the right hardware and software, the downloader can use the magnetic sequence to reproduce the sound recording. The electronic file (or, perhaps more accurately, the appropriate segment of the hard disk) is therefore a "phonorecord" within the meaning of the statute.

The ReDigi court also relied on prior cases regarding illegal file-sharing:

---

148 Id. at 170.
149 Id. at 171.

In addition to the reproduction right, a copyright owner also has the exclusive right "to distribute copies or phonorecords of the copyrighted work to the public by sale or other transfer of ownership." 17 U.S.C. § 106(3). Like the court in London–Sire, the Court agrees that "[a]n electronic file transfer is plainly within the sort of transaction that § 106(3) was intended to reach [and] ... fit[s] within the definition of 'distribution' of a phonorecord." London–Sire, 542 F.Supp.2d at 173–74. For that reason, "courts have not hesitated to find copyright infringement by distribution in cases of file-sharing or electronic transmission of copyrighted works." Arista Records LLC v. Greubel, 453 F.Supp.2d 961, 968 (N.D.Tex.2006) (collecting cases); see, e.g., Napster, 239 F.3d at 1014. Indeed, in New York Times Co., Inc. v. Tasini, the Supreme Court stated it was "clear" that an online news database violated authors' distribution rights by selling electronic copies of their articles for download. 533 U.S. 483, 498, 121 S.Ct. 2381, 150 L.Ed.2d 500 (2001).[150]

---

150 ReDigi at 652.

Chapter 23

●　　●　　●

WRAPPING UP THE NEW MUSIC PARADIGM

"I think people have been obsessed with the wrong question; that is 'How do we make people pay for music?' What if we started asking, 'How do we let people pay for music?'" - Amanda Palmer's TED talk from March 2013

The changes in the music industry have been seismic and it has affected everyone in both worlds of music. Both have seen declining album sales, including downloads, with the music now being almost a loss leader. Vinyl and cassette sales do remain strong though. While major artists get many more streams than indie artists, it still does not make up for lost album sales. Touring is the one thing that major artists can still do.

The conundrum for new artists is that while it has never been easier to record and release your own music, there is just so much of it out there and they get paid so little for it. It is harder to tour as well, and, even if you do, people may not buy your stuff because you are online. But, if you are not on the web, you may as well be invisible.

Radiohead's manager has called for a government investigation over the secret deals between the record labels and Spotify. The labels and Spotify have signed Non-Disclosure Agreements (NDA's), so they cannot legally reveal the terms of the deal. NDA's are very common amongst business partners. When I was general counsel for THECOOLTV, we signed them all the time with people we dealt with, intended to deal with, or just thought about working with.

We have come to the point where the album is a loss leader or just a way to get people in the door for touring, merchandise, or other revenue opportunities. Further, major label artists never make much from album sales because of one-sided contracts. They always must rely on alternative sources of income like touring, publishing, and merchandise to offset what their labels did not pay them in royalties. Lyle Lovett admitted that after selling over 4.6 million records he has received nothing in record royalties from his label. But he's had a very successful career. "I've never made a dime from a record sale in the history of my record deal. I've been very happy with my sales, and certainly my audience has been very supportive. I make a living going out and playing shows," says Lovett.

Because album sales are so depressed, record labels have had to find new ways to contractually extort money from artists. If you Google it, you can find a Lady Gaga contract showing exactly how major labels avoid paying anything to their artists from streaming services like Spotify. But it turns out there are a few more tricks for paying artists absolutely nothing while pocketing millions in streaming revenues.

In a report online on Digital Music News, according to Rich Bengloff, head of independent label group A2IM, these dirty tricks are currently being employed by Universal Music Group, which just happens to the be Lady Gaga's label. Bengloff spilled this three-step process to Billboard:

(1) "Universal Music makes the per-stream rate as low as they possibly can so they have to give the artist very little money."

(2) "Then, on top of that, they have something called a 'listener hour guarantee,' which they know is going to up their compensation by about 40% — since it's per listener hour, not per track, the artist gets screwed because it's not attributable to a track, so the artist doesn't get a royalty. That's not fair, that's not the way we do business."

(3) "The third thing they do is get a minimum annual guarantee or an advance if they know the service isn't going to reach that level of business and be able to recoup — it's what's called [digital] breakage and they also don't share that with the artists."

Now, I am not here to bash record labels. There are a lot of great independent and smaller labels. Even the majors serve their purpose—they do make stars out of some artists and allow them to live as artists. Even bands who are now on their own, like Radiohead and Pearl Jam, would never be where they are without the major labels they were once on.

Spotify has about 100 million active listeners, while Apple Music has about 15 million as they play catch up. Both sites have around 30 million songs in their catalog, but as of this writing, that data is probably outdated. SoundCloud has 175 million users, but this is a different model since artists upload their own music.

SoundCloud	175 million (Aug 2015)
Spotify	100 million (June 2016)
Pandora	77 million (Sept 2015)
NetEase Cloud Music (China)	55 million (May 2015)
iHeartRadio	48 million (July 2015)
Slacker	26 million (July 2015)
Apple Music	15 million (Oct 2015)
Amazon Prime	10 million (Aug 2015)

A very recent development as I write this book underscores the rise of streaming and the decline of record labels. A slew of mega-stars such as Drake, Beyonce, kanye West, and Frank Ocean have released albums exclusively on streaming sites such as Tidal and Apple Music. In Drake's case, Apple Music actually paid for exclusive music videos, thus, taking over a traditional role of record labels.

These exclusives have alienated a lot of music fans, however, Fans would have to sign up or pay to belong to multiple streaming services just to hear their favorite albums. Here are two examples that show how the tables have turned. First, Lady Gaga told her label that if they agreed to an exclusive release, she would start to leak tracks. The second example may be the most brazen I have ever seen. In August Frank Ocean released his long-awaited follow-up album, *Endless,* thus fulfilling his record deal with Def Jam/Universal. Ocean was not happy with his label, Then, very shortly thereafter, gave a superior album,

Blonde, as an exclusive to Apple Music. Jimmy Iovine, an experienced music business veteran, no doubt sees Apple Music as filling a void for artists who are on their own, but have brand names.[151]

Practice Tip: While uncommon for indie artists, the optimal scenario is to control all your copyrights and have a label just do the distribution for a percentage of sales. Because this is not possible for most artists, then a third party should be used as I have discussed.

Indie Record Stores

There are no more national record chains like Tower Records or Sam Goody. Walmart and Target carry a few select new CDs from mega sellers like Adele or Drake. WEA, Warner Music's distribution and marketing arm, has shut down the accounts of "about a hundred" retailers that did less than $10,000 in business with the company last year, a WEA source has confirmed to Pitchfork. The move put into effect an existing policy requiring a $10,000 minimum annual order for stores holding direct accounts with WEA. This could have a devastating effect on small record stores around the country, representatives for various shops tell Pitchfork.

However, while physical music sales in the U.S. has been declining for years (except vinyl), that is not the case around the world. Sales of physical music, particularly in Latin America (the fastest growing region in world), Germany, Japan, and China are increasing; globally, vinyl sales went up 55 percent in 2014, and accounted for 6% of ALL music sales which was the biggest piece of the sales pie since 1988.

Now that we have covered all the exclusive rights you get with the two copyrights in every song, including the new digital spectrum, it is time to wrap up some concepts. This is especially so given the amount and complexity of the info I have given you.

There are four types of royalties:

---

151 Rolling Stone Magazine, Oct. 20, 2016, pps. 13-14.

1.) A mechanical royalty

In the case of YouTube this can also be considered a synchronization royalty because the music is synchronized to a moving picture (video).

2.) A performance royalty

A performance royalty is owed to songwriters and/or publishers of a song whenever that composition is "broadcast" or performed "in public."

3) Sound Recording

An additional royalty for the sound recording is also generated, and this is a separate revenue stream from the composition royalty.

4) Licensing

This is when you license your song or sound recording for use in a TV show, movies, commercials, samples or replays. The publisher can also earn mechanicals from some of these.

If other people use your compositions on their videos on YouTube, YouTube will pay this money to the copyright owner, but only if you are represented by a publishing administrator. An administrator must register your compositions with YouTube for you to receive this money. One exception to this is for videos on your own YouTube channel. If you claim the compositions on your own channel, then you would receive the mechanical (synchronization) royalty directly from YouTube. Note that the performance uses for your self-owned videos would still go to the local collection agency (or PRO in the US). In general, if your compositions are not claimed, you do not receive the money. YouTube does not pay retroactively, so you must claim your compositions as soon as possible.

Outside of the U.S., these royalties are automatically paid to the various collection societies around the world, just like any other streaming service (e.g. Spotify). In most cases, without a publishing administrator you will not be able to receive this money. This happens for both the mechanical (sometimes defined as synchronization) and performance royalties. These societies pay this money to the copyright holders of the compositions. You must be registered by an administrator in their territory to receive your money. There are reciprocal agreements in place for the performance royalty between ASCAP,

BMI, and SESAC. However, this does not include the mechanical (synchronization) royalty.

Without a publishing administrator, you would only see the resulting performance money generated by third party videos IF your compositions are identified by the societies. A 2015 Berklee College of Music report found that anywhere from 20-50% of music payments do not make it to their rightful owners. The indie publishing powerhouse Kobalt calculated that there are more than 900,000 distinct royalty payments for artists and songwriters.

A Summation of Artist Royalties

Sound Recording Digital Performance Royalties
These come from non-interactive (programmed for you) digital platforms like Internet and satellite radio.

How to Get Paid: SoundExchange
Download Sales: These come from when someone downloads your music on iTunes, Google Play, Amazon, etc.

How to Get Paid: Your Distribution Company
Sites like Bandcamp and Loudr pay the artist directly because they are artist-managed stores.

Interactive Streaming Revenue
This royalty goes to the artist/label. While these services claim they pay out 70% of all revenue, the 70% is for both the artist/label revenue and the songwriter royalties (mechanicals). Streaming revenue to artists is much more than the mechanicals paid to songwriters.

How to Get Paid: Your Distribution Company
YouTube
YouTube can earn money for artists, and is how most younger music fans discover music, but it can be confusing. I study this stuff and

must constantly refresh myself because YouTube does not easily fit into a mechanical or public performance, often involves the use of moving images or pictures, and there's a lot of covers uploaded. With that in mind, let's dive in. According to a piece by The Guardian, an anonymous songwriter reported a profit of $80 for 9 million plays. YouTube also does not have performance rights agreements in every country with the service, so some views do not actually count toward royalties at all, but still bring in advertising money for YouTube.

Even in the U.K., where YouTube does have a deal with the Performance Rights Society, the video streaming company pays a lump sum for licensing, which is then distributed among songwriters. This model means that the popularity of a song makes little difference for royalties.

The best bet for generating a profit at YouTube is by generating enough views to become a premium partner and earning money through advertising. While YouTube is very useful for sharing music and especially live performances, don't go into it expecting to generate a significant profit.

YouTube Sound Recording Revenue

You can make money on any video that uses your sound recording, whether you recorded it or not, if you allow YouTube to put ads on the video. Either videos you upload or fan made dog videos with your sound recordings can generate ad revenue that you can collect. YouTube splits the ad revenue 45%/55% in your favor.

How to Get Paid: Most digital distribution companies have this option. If your distribution does not handle this, you can sign up for independent YouTube revenue collection companies like Audiam, AdRev or InDMusic. But it's easiest if you keep everything under one roof.

YouTube Composition Royalties

In addition to performance royalties, you can earn a percentage of the ad revenue generated from the video if it is your composition. Your admin publishing company will handle this. YouTube's Content ID program does not catch every time your song is played, unfortunately. Some admin publishing companies and YouTube collections companies are better at tracking than others, so do your homework. Some do manual searches/listen. Others have different systems in place. You can always ask your company how they do it.

Facebook also is getting into the video space, and is gaining on YouTube. Since June 2014, Facebook video has averaged 1 billion views a day with over 65% of the views worldwide happening on mobile. In just one year the number of video posts per person has increased 75% globally and 94% in the U.S. As of now though, there is no way to monetize your videos on Facebook; so, it is only for exposure, not cash for the artist. Approximately two-thirds of adult Internet users around the world stream music at least once a month, but just one in 10 digital consumers pay for streaming music, according to a GlobalWebIndex study.

But the news is not all bad, as the study found that people age 16 to 24 were the most likely to purchase a subscription to a music streaming service. This creates a tremendous revenue opportunity for companies that can convince younger users to sign up because it generates stable and long-term revenue streams as these young users grow older and form habits around the service.

Digital Distribution

There are so many places for artists to put their music online, it can be over-whelming. Different websites offer different packages for bands, and there are new websites popping up all the time.

Bandcamp

The structure of the site allows for easy downloading as well as stream-ing, and Bandcamp allows bands to name any price for a download. Customers are also able to buy physical releases and merch from a band, listed underneath the digital option.

Bandcamp's payment program is simple: the company takes 10 percent of merch sales and 15 percent of downloads. After a seller reaches a $5,000 profit, Bandcamp's cut drops to 10 percent of digital profit. Revenue is linked to a seller's PayPal account, so that $5,000 can come from any number of releases and artists directed to the same PayPal account.

For $10 a month, an artist can upgrade to a Bandcamp Pro account, allowing the seller to send out discount codes, use private streaming options and access in depth analytics. The only downside is that no revenue is generated from album streams, so an artist only makes money when someone buys an album or download.

SoundCloud

Free accounts are allowed only two hours of upload time, so to get the most out of SoundCloud, you're going to have shell out some money up front. A Pro account costs $6 a month or $55 a year and allows for four hours' worth of uploads. An Unlimited account costs $15 a month or $135 a year, and as you'd expect, allows for unlimited uploads, though users are only allowed to add 30 hours of music each week.

The paid accounts allow for more downloads, analytics and let a user spotlight five songs at the top of his or her profile. Pro and Unlimited users can also turn on Quiet Mode, making comments and statistics private.

However, SoundCloud does not directly pay royalties for streams. If you're looking to get paid for streams, you'll have to partner up with non-profit SoundExchange and license your music, making SoundCloud more of a tool for sharing rather than selling. Links to iTunes can be included as a Buy button, however.

Pandora

According to Pandora, one million plays result in about $1,370. That money is then divided amongst the label, songwriters and performers, which makes for a very small sum of money awarded to each musician. Getting your music on Pandora requires that your music already be on a service such as iTunes or Bandcamp, and like Spotify, royalties can be collected through a label or SoundExchange.

iTunes

iTunes has long been a dominant distribution medium for music—relying on downloads more than streaming—and getting music on the program is fairly streamlined. However, for smaller artists, the costs can sometimes trump the benefits. Most artists must use a third party distributor like TuneCore or CD Baby to get music posted. iTunes then takes approximately 30 percent of sales from music. While this is a bit more costly than other services, the popularity of iTunes does make it an appealing service. Downloads from iTunes also easily go onto an iPod or other device, which makes music more readily accessible for fans.

Other Options

Rdio, Beats Music, Rhapsody, Napster and Google Play Music, work on a similar model to Spotify, but the latter four don't have a freemium model, meaning royalty payments are typically higher (accounting from an anonymous indie label shows Google Play paying nine times what Spotify pays—even Rdio shows a significant per-stream increase from Spotify). Deezer also works similarly to Spotify and is available in nearly 200 countries—just not the U.S. Slacker Rdio and Samsung's new Milk Music operate more like Pandora. Using a service like SoundExchange can earn royalties from the likes of iHeartRadio and SiriusXM, as well as Pandora. Xbox Music, while relatively small compared to the other services on this list, has become known for paying much higher royalties than its peers.

DistroKid is also a digital distribution company, and they are the only one who can send payments to multiple parties like a producer, co-writer, or other members of the band. This can be a big deal if you're in a band, and particularly if you split money depending on the song. But, there's one **huge** caveat—this only applies to sound recording royalties, not composition royalties, so this gets only half (or less) of the pie divided.

So, if you distribute your music with a digital distribution company that does not have a publishing component, and you wrote the songs, the only way to collect all your songwriting royalties is via an admin publishing company like SongTrust, Audiam or Kobalt. Your PRO (ASCAP, BMI, SESAC, SOCAN) does not collect all your songwriting royalties - only performance royalties.

Sources of Revenue for Musicians

1. Sales of physical music: While CD sales are slumping, vinyl and cassette sales are increasing.

2. Digital Sales: You will make the most through your website, but you can, and should, use iTunes, Bandcamp, Amazon, and a host of other sites that sell downloads.

3. Streaming: While the pay is low, you are exposing your music, and the pay may get better in the future.

4. Live Shows: Money made from live shows can vary greatly, but it's still one of the best ways to earn income. Not only can you make money from selling tickets, but it's also one of the best ways to sell merch and physical music.

5. Physical Merch: The more you tour, the more you sell. This can run the gamut from concert t-shirts to stickers to coffee mugs. While I don't talk a lot about this in this book, if you are serious, get a logo and use it as your brand and put it on everything. You should also get it trademarked.

6. Digital Merch: You can also sell digital merch items like PDFs, videos, and images to your fans. Things like lyric books, live concerts, sheet music, exclusive photos, and artwork. This is a chance for an artist to use their creativity.

7. Crowdfunding: Another topic that I do not delve into much here, but there's a lot of info online, and sites like Patreon and Kickstarter can help artists with projects such as completing an album, shooting a video and others discussed above. More on this below.

8. Publishing Royalties: All the revenue sources we have discussed that come from the music composition.

9. Digital Royalties: All revenue generated from sound recordings via SoundExchange.

10. Live Performance Royalties: These are not overwhelming, but when you (or someone else) perform live a song you wrote, you can get paid.

11. Licensing: You can get paid for the use of either your music composition, sound recording, or both if you own both, when your song is

used in a TV show, commercial or movie. This is easier said than done, but it is out there as we discussed, and YouTube offers opportunities for this as well.

12. YouTube: On YouTube, whenever your music is used in videos that are running ads, YouTube pays a portion of that advertising money to the rights holders of the song and/or sound recording owner. Digital distributors like TuneCore and CD Baby can help you collect that money, as well as Audiam.

It is impossible to separate music copyright law, changing technology, and the music business. There is a rapper named Nipsey Hussle who used to be on a label and now releases his music on his own. The old paradigm in the music industry has changed. Musicians need to develop their own. Hussle believes that all digital music should be free, but he charges $1,000 per album, with the caveat that there's only 100 issued and they come with special features.

According to Hussle, "digital music is abundant and it's going against the laws of nature to charge for something that is ubiquitous. It would be like charging for air." And his view of the record industry? "The labels aren't letting us live. They're not letting artists own anything! We're going to end up 60 years old without a pot to piss in – no catalogue, no mailbox money, no residuals."

As should be evident by now, with the increase in streaming, and decrease in music sales, money for most songwriters is drying up. Album sales peaked in 2000, with 785 million albums sold. In 2014, Americans bought just 257 million albums, a decrease of 305% over that period.

There are more places for musicians to sell and promote their music, yet most do not pay much and there's so much music out there. Musicians need to know that iTunes takes a 30% cut and gives the artist no info on who is buying your record. While I still think musicians need to have their music on iTunes, they should also be on sites like Bandcamp, Loudr, and Bandcamp and CD Baby provide bands customer data. Now, putting the music on your own website (or selling it at shows) ensures the most profit, but driving traffic to the site is always an issue.

The lesson: Have your music distribution diversified to reach as many people as possible on as many platforms as possible.

There are several websites that allow artists to reach out to fans and potential fans. Kickstarter, PledgeMusic, Indiegogo and Patreon have allowed artists to offer high priced rewards/exclusives to diehard fans. Patreon's model allows artists to monetize these fans on an ongoing basis. BandPage offers experiences enabling artists to monetize their most ardent fans in creative ways while on tour. Bandcamp and Loudr allow fans to name their price for downloads. Fanswell allows artists to easily set up house concert tours to make the most money from a small, but dedicated fan base.

10 Rules for Artists

1. Have an operating agreement.
2. Register as a business.
3. Treat yourself as a tax entity.
4. There are two copyrights in every song.
5. Own your masters.
6. Never give away your publishing.
7. Register your songs and sound recordings.
8. Register a whole album as a collective work if you can.
9. Get digital distribution and publishing via a third party.
10. Register your sound recordings via SoundExchange and join a PRO.

Money streams summary

1) PROs collect public performance royalties, including non-interactive streaming.

2) Harry Fox collects MR on reproduction, including interactive streaming.

3) Sound Exchange collects sound recording royalties.

If you are a songwriter or rights holder, get all the $$$ you entitled to:

1) Get digital distribution and publishing via a 3rd party.

2) Join a PRO to collect performance revenue.

3) Join Sound Exchange to collect sound recording royalties.

MEDIUM	EXAMPLE	MECHANICALS	WHO SETS RATE ON MECHANICALS	WHO COLLECTS ON MECHANICALS	PUBLIC PERFORMANCE	WHO SETS RATE ON PUBLIC PERFORMANCE	WHO COLLECTS ON PUBLIC PERFORMANCE	SOUND RECORDING	WHO SETS RATE ON SOUND RECORDING	WHO COLLECTS ON SOUND RECORDING
Terrestrial Radio	WSRT, Chicago, NUT Austin	No	N/A	N/A	Yes	Statutory, set by CRB; DOJ regulates	PROs who paid on to publishers	No	N/A	N/A
Interactive Streaming	Spotify	Yes	Copyright Rate Board (CRB)	HF A/Publishers/3rd party	Yes	PROs negotiate, DOJ regulate	PROs who paid on to publishers/3rd party	Yes	Negotiate	SoundExchange (SE)/3rd party
Non-interactive Streaming	Pandora	No	N/A	N/A	Yes	PROs negotiate, DOJ regulate	PROs who paid on to publishers/3rd party	Yes	Negotiate	SE or third party
Video Streaming	YouTube	Yes	Negotiate, CRB-no authority here	HF A/Publishers/3rd party	Yes	PROs negotiate, DOJ regulate	PROs who paid on to publishers/3rd party	Yes	Negotiate	SE or third party

SECTION FOUR

• • •

COPYRIGHT INFRINGEMENT CASES

Chapter 24

● ● ●

INTRODUCTION TO COPYRIGHT CASES

We have been through all the rights you get with a copyright, but what if you feel someone has violated your rights? What if you feel someone infringes upon your copyright, has appropriated your work without getting permission, or subconsciously has "stolen" your song? While not common, these types of cases generate a lot of headline news, from George Harrison's "My Sweet Lord" to Robin Thicke's "Blurred Lines."

Let me note at the outset that the following discussion involves the copyright infringement of the music (song), not the sound recording. You can, of course, violate the sound recording copyright as discussed previously. For example, using a master recording in a sample without permission.

The scope of inquiry is much narrower when the work in question is a sound recording. The only issue is whether the actual sound recording has been used without authorization. Substantial similarity is not generally an issue. Certainly, with modern recording technology, this may be hard to tell at times. Keep in mind you can infringe either (or both) the musical composition or the sound recording.[152]

---

152 See Erickson v. Blake, 839 F. Supp. 2d 1132, 1135 n.3 (D. Or. 2012) ("Sound recordings and musical compositions are separate works with their own distinct copyrights.") We discussed sound recording infringement when I discussed sampling, so this section is devoted to infringing the musical composition primarily.

Preliminary Matters
Jurisdiction and Venue

The Copyright Act provides federal district courts original and exclusive jurisdiction over federal statutory copyright cases.[153] Federal jurisdiction is exclusive when invoking a statutory copyright under Title 17. Keep in mind that much of copyright law is amended contractually, and state courts typically have jurisdiction over contract disputes.

The pertinent venue provision of the United States Code provides that civil actions relating to copyrights may be instituted in the district in which the defendant or his agent resides or may be found.[154]

Under the Copyright Act of 1976, only parties with ownership rights in a copyright have standing to bring claims for its infringement.[155] As the owner of "an exclusive right under a copyright," an exclusive licensee is "entitled ... to institute an action for any infringement of that particular right committed while he or she is the owner of it."[156]

The upshot is that a plaintiff need not be the same party who initially registered the subject work. Any other rule would necessitate redundant registrations for standing purposes every time legal and beneficial ownership of rights were transferred.[157]

Led Zeppelin Case

In 2014, Led Zeppelin was sued by the estate of Randy Wolfe, the late leader of the band Spirit. The plaintiffs sued in the Eastern District of Pennsylvania and alleged that Zeppelin's "Stairway to Heaven," released in 1971, infringed on Spirit's "Taurus." The two songs have a similar opening.

---

153 28 U.S.C. 1338(a).

154 Venue is governed by 28 USC 1400(a): "civil actions, suits, or proceedings arising under any Act of Congress relating to copyrights or exclusive rights in mask works or designs may be instituted in the district in which the defendant or his agent resides or may be found."

155 See Latin Am. Mech. Rights Collection Agency, Inc. v. Marti, Flores, Prieto & Wachtel Adver., Inc., 204 F. Supp. 2d 270, 271 (D.P.R. 2002).

156 17 U.S.C. § 501(b); Eden Toys, Inc. v. Florelee Undergarment Co., 697 F.2d 27 (2d Cir. 1982).

157 Smith v. Casey, 741 F.3d 1236, 1243 (11th Cir. 2014).

On May 6, 2015, Defendants Led Zeppelin moved to either dismiss for lack of jurisdiction or transfer the case to the United States District Court for the Central District of California from the Eastern District of Pennsylvania.[158] The court said that the Pennsylvania court did not have either general or specific personal jurisdiction over the defendants (Federal Rules of Civil Procedure 12(b)). The tests for both general and specific jurisdiction were described by the court in Skidmore v. Zeppelin:

> For general jurisdiction to exist, "the contacts between the defendant and the forum need not be specifically related to the underlying cause of action," Pinker v. Roche Holdings Ltd., 292 F.3d 361, 368 n.1 (3d Cir. 2002), but "only a limited set of affiliations with a forum will render a defendant amenable to all-purpose jurisdiction there," Daimler AG v. Bauman, 134 S. Ct. 746, 760, 187 L. Ed. 2d 624 (2014). For an individual, "the paradigm forum for the exercise of general jurisdiction is the individual's domicile," id. (quoting Goodyear, 131 S. Ct. at 2853-54), and for a corporation, the paradigm fora are its "place of incorporation and principal place of business," id. The Supreme Court has made clear that only in an "exceptional case" would an individual be "essentially at home" in a forum other that of its domicile. Id. at 761 n.19.
>
> For specific jurisdiction, the Third Circuit typically applies a three-part test: First, the defendant must have purposefully directed [its] activities at the forum. Second, the litigation must arise out of or relate to at least one of those activities. And third, if the prior two requirements are met, a court may consider whether the exercise of jurisdiction otherwise comport[s] with fair play and substantial justice. O'Connor, 496 F.3d at 317.[159]

---

158 The only apparent reason that plaintiff's lawyer chose this venue is that he lived or offices in this federal district.

159 Skidmore v. Led Zeppelin, (unpublished so far - Westlaw citation: 2015 WL 2116632; Lexis citation: 2015 LEXIS 59113).

In the Zeppelin case, the court found that the Eastern District of Pennsylvania did not have jurisdiction over the defendants, therefore rendering the venue improper. The defendants moved to either dismiss or move the claims. The court chose to transfer the claims, rather than dismiss them, as the defendants consented to personal jurisdiction in the Central District of California.

Statute of Limitations

"'A cause of action for copyright infringement accrues when one has knowledge of a violation or is chargeable with such knowledge.'[160] In a case of continued infringement, however, 'an action may be brought for all acts that accrued within the three years preceding the filing of the suit.'"[161]

The statute of limitation provisions in copyright infringement cases is found in 17 USC 507(a) and (b), and is three years in a civil action, and 5 years in a criminal proceeding. "No civil action shall be maintained under the provisions of this title unless it is commenced within three years after the claim accrued."[162] So long as the action is timely "commenced," there is no bar to introducing relevant evidence from the time-period before the statute of limitations accrued.[163]

Over the years, Courts have been split between a continuing violation, where there is really no statute of limitations, versus going back only three years. The latter doctrine is the majority view. "Application of the continuous wrong doctrine generally has been rejected in the infringement context."[164] The prevailing view, therefore, is that the statute of limitations bars recovery on any damage claim that accrued over three years prior to filing of suit.[165]

The circuits have treated ongoing copyright violations differently. In Taylor v. Merick,[166] the 7th Circuit gave weight to what is called the "con-

---

160 Riley v. New World Pictures, Ltd., 19 F.3d 479, 481 (9th Cir. 1994).

161 Id. Kourts v. Cameron, 419 F.3d 989, 999 (9th Cir. 2005).

162 17 U.S.C. 507(B).

163 See Arista Records LLC v. Lime Group LLC, 784 F. Supp. 2d 398, 418 (S.D.N.Y. 2011

164 Stone v. Williams, 970 F.2d 1043, 1050 (2d Cir. 1992), cert. denied, 508 U.S. 906 (1993).

165 Polar Bear Prods., Inc. v. Timex Corp., 384 F.3d 700, 706 (9th Cir. 2004).

166 712 F.2d 1112 (7th Cir. 1983),

tinuing violation" doctrine. In Taylor, the court said that "the statute of limitations does not begin to run on a copyright claim involving a continuing series of copyright infringements until the entire series is over and done with."[167] When a court recognizes the continuing violation doctrine, a plaintiff is able to recover for all infringements if the final infringing act is brought within 3 years. However, as stated above, that doctrine is rejected in other circuits or applied in very limited circumstances. Even the 7th Circuit has limited the Taylor holding. The problem with the continuing violation theory is that it could lead to a situation in which there is no statute of limitations for sound recordings violations. If you re-mix or master a sound recording, it is a new sound recording. This has the effect of extending the copyright, thus extending the statute of limitations. For example, Led Zeppelin re-mastered their entire catalog, including "Stairway to Heaven." Thus, plaintiffs could argue that this begins a new running of the statute of limitations.[168]

Raging Bull Case

In a 6-3 majority opinion by Justice Ruth Bader Ginsburg, the high court held that the equitable defense of laches cannot be invoked to preclude damages claims brought within the applicable three-year statute of limitations.

> "The expansive role for laches MGM envisions careens away from understandings, past and present, of the essentially gap-filling, not legislation-overriding, office of laches," writes Justice Ginsburg in her opinion. "Nothing in this Court's precedent suggests a doctrine of such sweep. Quite the contrary, we have never applied laches to bar in their entirety claims for discrete wrongs occurring within a federally

---

167 Taylor at 1119.

168 "In Cain v. Universal Pictures Co., 47 F.Supp. 1013 (S.D.Cal. 1942), the Court held that acts of infringement continued while a motion picture was being exhibited. There one of the defendants was a script writer for the film. Judge Yankwich concluded that although the writer's direct activity ceased with the delivery of the script, as it was intended that the script would be the basis for the film and the film would be shown continuously, the script writer's infringement carried on while the film was on exhibition." Baxter v. Curtis Indus., Inc., 201 F.Supp 100, 101 (N.D. Ohio 1962).

prescribed limitations period. Inviting individual judges to set a time limit other than the one Congress prescribed, we note, would tug against the uniformity Congress sought to achieve when it enacted §507(b)."

"It is hardly incumbent on copyright owners, however, to challenge each and every actionable infringement," she writes in explaining why a plaintiff might not sue right away. "And there is nothing untoward about waiting to see whether an infringer's exploitation undercuts the value of the copyrighted work, has no effect on the original work, or even complements it... If the rule were, as MGM urges, 'sue soon, or forever hold your peace," copyright owners would have to mount a federal case fast to stop seemingly innocuous infringements, lest those infringements eventually grow in magnitude."

The majority decision described the Copyright Act's statute of limitations as "a three-year look-back limitations period for all civil claims arising under the Copyright Act," and then labeled the time "when a copyright infringement claim accrues" as "when a plaintiff has a complete and present cause of action." Given the posture of the case before it as one for infringement, the Court immediately added that a copyright claim "accrues when an infringing act occurs."

The Court noted that nine Courts of Appeal employ the discovery rule rather than the injury rule to make that determination, but added that "we have not passed on the question." But the opinion did overtly side with the separate-accrual rule rather than the continuing wrong approach, citing Stone v. Williams for the proposition that "each infringing act starts a new limitations period." It explained that, against a defendant who has engaged in a series of discrete infringing acts, "the copyright holder's suit ordinarily will be timely under § 507(b) with respect to more recent acts of infringement (i.e., acts within the three-year window), but untimely with respect to prior acts of the same or similar kind."

It should here be recalled that no action for copyright infringement may be brought until application is made to register the subject work in the

Copyright Office except for works of foreign origin.[169] Once registration has been effectuated, action may be instituted for infringements that occurred before, as well as after, its effective date.[170] Unless the question is purely one of law, plaintiffs have the right to a jury trial.

---

169 Goebel v. Manis, 39 F. Supp. 2d 1318, 1319 (D. Kan. 1999); See Nimmer 7.16[B][1][b]
170 Eden Toys, Inc. v. Florelee Undergarment Co., 697 F.2d 27 (2d Cir. 1982).

Chapter 25

● ● ●

WHAT A PLAINTIFF MUST PROVE

In establishing a claim of copyright infringement of a musical composition, the plaintiff must prove (1) ownership of the copyright in the complaining work; (2) originality of the work; (3) copying of the work by the defendant (access to the work), and (4) a substantial or striking degree of similarity between the two works.[171] Thus, there are two threshold matters—possession of the copyright (usually publishers own the copyright) and that the song is "original." As I show below, originality is a low bar—simply that you created the song and did not copy it. Therefore, in order to prevail, a plaintiff has the burden of showing two main things: access and substantial or striking similarity between the songs in question.

Plaintiff's ownership, in turn, breaks down into the following: (1) originality in the author; (2) copyrightability of the subject matter; (3) a national point of attachment of the work, such as to permit a claim of copyright; (4) compliance with applicable statutory formalities; and (5) (if the plaintiff is not the author) a transfer of rights or other relationship between the author and the plaintiff so as to constitute the plaintiff as the valid copyright claimant. A copyright certificate provides prima facie evidence of the above. A plaintiff's

---

171 Selle v. Brothers Gibb, 567 F.Supp. 1173 (N.Ill 1983) aff'd 741 F.2d 896, 900 (7th Cir. 1984) (hereafter Selle). See Sherman, Musical Copyright Infringement: The Requirement of Substantial Similarity. Copyright Law Symposium, Number 92, American Society of Composers, Authors and Publishers 81-82. Columbia University Press (1977) [hereinafter Sherman].

case fails without showing the defendant appropriated anything or if defendant can prove the work was independently created.

Originality

It is well-established that the originality requirement for obtaining a copyright is an extremely low threshold, unlike the novelty requirement for securing a patent. Originality for copyright purposes amounts to "... little more than a prohibition of actual copying." No matter how poor the "author's' addition, it is enough if it be his own."[172] Although slavish copying involving no artistic skill whatsoever does not qualify, a showing of virtually any independent creativity will do.[173]

Access

The infringer must have had access to the song (i.e., they could likely hear it); after all, you presumably cannot copy something you have not heard. Access requires evidence rather than a mere possibility of hearing it through conjecture or speculation.[174]

In the early 1980s, the Bee Gees were sued for copyright infringement for their hit from the movie *Saturday Night Fever*, "How Deep Is Your Love." I discuss the case below, but here's an extended quote from Selle v. Brothers Gibb regarding access and its close relationship with the substantial similarity prong.

> You can prove access if something is so strikingly similar. If, however, the plaintiff does not have direct evidence of access, then an inference of access may still be established circumstantially by proof of

---

172 Alfred Bell & Co. v. Catalda Fine Arts, Inc., 191 F.2d 99, 103 (2d Cir.1951) (citation omitted).

173 See Durham Industries, Inc. v. Tomy Corp., 630 F.2d 905 (2d Cir.1980); L. Batlin & Son, Inc. v. Snyder, 536 F.2d 486 (2d Cir.) (in banc), cert. denied, 429 U.S. 857 (1976).

174 Scott v. Paramount Pictures Corp., 449 F. Supp. 518, 520 (D.C.D.C.1978) aff'd, 197 U.S. App. D.C. 180, 607 F.2d 494 (D.C.Cir.1979), cert. denied, 449 U.S. 849, 101 S. Ct. 137, 66 L. Ed. 2d 60 (1980); see 3 Nimmer on Copyright § 13.02[A], p. 13-12 (1982).

similarity which is so striking that the possibilities of independent creation, coincidence and prior common source are, as a practical matter precluded. If the plaintiff presents evidence of striking similarity sufficient to raise an inference of access, then copying is presumably proved simultaneously, although the fourth element (substantial similarity) still requires proof that the defendant copied a substantial amount of the complaining work. The theory which Selle attempts to apply to this case is based on proof of copying by circumstantial proof of access established by striking similarity between the two works.

One difficulty with plaintiff's theory is that no matter how great the similarity between the two works, it is not their similarity per se which establishes access; rather, their similarity tends to prove access in light of the nature of the works, the particular musical genre involved and other circumstantial evidence of access. In other words, striking similarity is just one piece of circumstantial evidence tending to show access and must not be considered in isolation; it must be considered together with other types of circumstantial evidence relating to access.

As a threshold matter, therefore, it would appear that there must be at least some other evidence which would establish a reasonable possibility that the complaining work was available to the alleged infringer. As noted, two works may be identical in every detail, but, if the alleged infringer created the accused work independently or both works were copied from a common source in the public domain, then there is no infringement. Therefore, if the plaintiff admits to having kept his or her creation under lock and key, it would seem logically impossible to infer access through striking similarity. Thus, although it has frequently been written that striking similarity alone can establish access, the decided cases suggest that this circumstance would be most unusual. The plaintiff must always present sufficient evidence to support a reasonable possibility of access because the jury cannot draw an inference of access based upon speculation and conjecture alone.[175]

---

175 Selle at 741 F.2d at 901.

Some cases, such as the one above, suggest that the stronger the similarity, the lower the bar is to prove access. This gets complicated though because most modern pop and rock songs are built upon very common chords which generally cannot be copyrighted. More on this later, but another wrench in the access prong is how ubiquitous music is today—it is seemingly everywhere. The possibility of a defendant hearing a plaintiff's song may be greater because of YouTube, Spotify, and all the other places to listen to music. However, it may be difficult to prove the defendant heard a particular song when it only got played a few hundred times on a particular website. Certainly, if the plaintiff's song was a big hit, it is usually easier to prove access, and vice versa.

Access can be a moving target depending on what Circuit you are in:

In this Circuit [2d], the test for proof of access in cases of striking similarity is less rigorous. In Arnstein v. Porter, 154 F.2d 464 (2d Cir.1946), Judge Frank said, "In some cases, the similarities between the plaintiff's and defendant's work are so extensive and striking as, without more, both to justify an inference of copying and to prove improper appropriation." Id. at 468-69 (emphasis added); see also Ferguson v. National Broadcasting Co., supra, 584 F.2d at 113 ("If the two works are so strikingly similar as to preclude the possibility of independent creation, 'copying' may be proved without a showing of access."); 3 M. & D. Nimmer, supra, § 13.02[B], at 13-17 (criticizing the Selle requirement that there be a "reasonable possibility" of access-not just a "bare possibility"-even in cases of striking similarity).

Appellants contend that undue reliance on striking similarity to show access precludes protection for the author who independently creates a similar work. However, the jury is only permitted to infer access from striking similarity; it need not do so. Though striking similarity alone can raise an inference of copying, that inference must be reasonable in light of all the evidence. A plaintiff has not proved striking similarity sufficient to sustain a finding of copying if the evidence as a whole does not preclude any reasonable possibility of independent creation. See Arnstein v. Porter, supra, 154 F.2d at 468

("If evidence of access is absent, the similarities must be so striking as to preclude the possibility that plaintiff and defendant independently arrived at the same result."); Ferguson v. National Broadcasting Co., supra, 584 F.2d at 113.[176]

One court held that a party can establish access either by demonstrating that (1) the infringed work has been widely disseminated; or (2) a particular chain of events exists by which the alleged infringer might have gained access to the copyright work.[177] There has to be reasonable possibility of access, not a bare one. Even if there is a "striking" similarity (higher proof than substantial), access may not be inferred via the Selle case if the song that is striking is commonplace or commonly found in similar works, such as common chord changes, or a prior common source.

Substantial Similarity

Even though there is overlap between the access and similarity prongs, the similarity prong should only be addressed after access is established. Similarity is the real meat of what it takes to prove a copyright infringement case—there must be a "substantial or striking similarity" between the songs in question.[178] Now, saying that is easier than defining or proving it, other than "you know it when you hear it."

Sherman defines "striking similarity" as a term of art signifying "that degree of similarity as will permit an inference of copying even in the absence of proof of access. . .."[179] Nimmer states that, absent proof of access, "the similarities must be so striking as to preclude the possibility that the defendant independently arrived at the same result."[180]

---

176 Gasie v. Kaiserman, 863 F.2d 106,1067-8 (2d Cir 1988).
177 Repp v. Lloyd Webber, 947 F. Supp. 105, 114 (S.D.N.Y. 1996) (citations omitted).
178 Marcoux v. Van Wyk, 572 F.2d 651, 653 (8th Cir.1978); see also 567 F.Supp. at 1183.
179 Sherman, Musical Copyright Infringement, at 84 n.15.
180 Nimmer at 13-14.4

"Striking similarity" is not merely a function of the number of identical notes that appear in both compositions.[181] An important factor in analyzing the degree of similarity of two compositions is the uniqueness of the sections which are asserted to be similar. The judicially formulated definition of "striking similarity" states that "plaintiffs must demonstrate that 'such similarities are of a kind that can only be explained by copying, rather than by coincidence, independent creation, or prior common source.'"[182]

Sherman adds that to prove certain similarities are "striking," plaintiff must show they are the sort of similarities that cannot satisfactorily be accounted for by a theory of coincidence, independent creation, prior common source, or any theory other than that of copying. Striking similarity is an extremely technical issue—one in which, understandably, experts are best equipped to deal with.[183]

To elaborate further on what experts need to prove and the relationship between access and striking or substantial similarity, one court stated:

In addition, to bolster the expert's conclusion that independent creation was not possible, there should be some testimony or other evidence of the relative complexity or uniqueness of the two compositions. In a field such as popular music in which all songs are relatively short and tend to build on or repeat a basic theme, such testimony would seem to be particularly necessary. We agree with the Sixth Circuit which explained that "we do not think the affidavit of [the expert witness], stating in conclusory terms that 'it is extremely unlikely that one set [of architectural plans] could have been prepared without access to the other set,' can fill the gap which is created by

---

181 Cf. Wilkie v. Santly Brothers, Inc., 13 F. Supp. 136 (S.D.N.Y. 1935), aff'd, 91 F.2d 978 (2d Cir.), cert. denied, 302 U.S. 735, 82 L. Ed. 568, 58 S. Ct. 120 (1937), aff'd on reargument, 94 F.2d 1023 (2d Cir. 1938) (comparison of note structure demonstrates striking similarity), and Jewel Music Publishing Co. v. Leo Feist, Inc., 62 F. Supp. 596 (S.D.N.Y. 1945) (in light of plaintiff's inability to establish access, degree of similarity despite identity or near identity of several bars was not striking).

182 Testa v. Janssen, 492 F. Supp. 198, 203 (W.D. Pa. 1980) (quoting Stratchborneo v. Arc Music Corp., 357 F. Supp. 1393, 1403 (S.D.N.Y. 1973)).

183 Sherman at 96.

the absence of any direct evidence of access." Scholz Homes, Inc. v. Maddox, 379 F.2d 84, 86 (6th Cir. 1967).

At oral argument, plaintiff's attorney analyzed the degree of similarity required to establish an inference of access as being in an inverse ratio to the quantum of direct evidence adduced to establish access. While we have found no authoritative support for this analysis, it seems appropriate. In this case, it would therefore appear that, because the plaintiff has introduced virtually no direct evidence of access, the degree of similarity required to establish copying in this case is considerable.

Under our case law, substantial similarity is inextricably linked to the issue of access. In what is known as the "inverse ratio rule," we "require a lower standard of proof of substantial similarity when a high degree of access is shown."[184]

Proof of substantial similarity is satisfied by a two-part test of extrinsic and intrinsic similarity.[185] Initially, the extrinsic test requires the plaintiff identify concrete elements based on objective criteria.[186] The extrinsic test often requires analytical dissection of a work and expert testimony.[187] Once the extrinsic test is satisfied, the fact-finder applies the intrinsic test. The intrinsic test is subjective and asks "whether the ordinary, reasonable person would find the total concept and feel of the works to be substantially similar."[188] If both the extrinsic and intrinsic elements of the test are satisfied, the works are said to be substantially similar.

---

184 Smith, 84 F.3d at 1218 (citing Shaw v. Lindheim, 919 F.2d 1353, 1361-62 (9th Cir. 1990); Krofft, 562 F.2d at 1172).

185 See Krofft, 562 F.2d at 1164.

186 See Smith, 84 F.3d at 1218; Shaw, 919 F.2d at 1356.

187 See Apple Computer, Inc v. Microsoft Corp., 35 F.3d 1435, 1442 (9th Cir. 1994).

188 Pasillas v. McDonald's Corp., 927 F.2d 440, 442 (9th Cir. 1991) (internal quotations omitted).

After establishing reasonable access and substantial similarity, a copyright plaintiff creates a presumption of copying. The burden shifts then to the defendant to rebut that presumption through proof of independent creation.[189]

Courts have also acknowledged the difficulty in defining what is "substantial or striking similarity."

> As courts and commentators have repeatedly noted, the test for substantial similarity is difficult to define and vague to apply, see Nimmer, § 13.03[A] at 13–27 (citing cases); Universal Athletic at 907 ("most cases are decided on an ad hoc basis"); Peter Pan Fabrics, Inc. v. Martin Weiner Corp., 274 F.2d 487, 489 (2d Cir.1960) ("[t]he test for infringement of a copyright is of necessity vague"). Nonetheless, it is repeatedly said that the test to determine substantial similarity is the response of the ordinary lay person. Universal Athletic at 907 (citing Arnstein v. Porter, 154 F.2d 464 (2d Cir.1946)).[190]

Thus, infringement based on fragmented literal similarity depends on whether "the value of a work may be substantially diminished even when only a part of it is copied, if the part that is copied is of great qualitative importance to the work as a whole."[191] Since it is not unlawful to copy non-copyrightable portions of a plaintiff's work, non-copyrightable elements must be factored out in an inquiry into infringement.[192] The policy supporting this rule is to prevent a deterring effect on the creation of new works because of authors' fears of copying innocuous segments.[193]

---

189 See Granite Music Corp. v. United Artists Corp., 532 F.2d 718, 721 (9th Cir. 1976). For a great summary of the above, see Three Boys Music Corp. v. Bolton, 1996 U.S. Dist. Lexis 22960 (C.D. CA 1996) aff'd 212 F.3d 477 (9th Cir. 2000).

190 Jarvis v. A & M Records, 827 F.Supp. 282, 290 (D.N.J. 1993).

191 Jarvis at 291.

192 See Warner Brothers v. American Broadcasting Companies, 720 F.2d 231, 240 (2d Cir.1983) ("a court may determine non-infringement as a matter of law on a motion for summary judgment ... [when] the similarity between two works concerns only non-copyrightable elements of the plaintiff's work....").

193 Warner Brothers at 240; Jarvis at 291.

While rare, it is possible to independently create something that is substantially similar to another work without copying it. There is no infringement if there is no copying.[194] This becomes more probable given the limited number of chords used in most rock and pop songs. However, this does present a conundrum. Say, for example, that you independently create something. If the plaintiff's song is a big hit, you may have a hard time arguing that you did indeed independently create your song.

Again, while not common, it is also not infringement if both parties copied from a prior common source—in music either a song or sound recording. Copyright infringement must be more than de minimis, though certainly that is hard to define. This potentially is powerful in the internet age where copyright infringements are commonplace.

> Parents in Central Park photograph their children perched on Jose de Creeft's Alice in Wonderland sculpture. We record television programs aired while we are out, so as to watch them at a more convenient hour. Waiters at a restaurant sing "Happy Birthday" at a patron's table. When we do such things, it is not that we are breaking the law but unlikely to be sued given the high cost of litigation. Because of the de minimis doctrine, in trivial instances of copying, we are in fact not breaking the law. If a copyright owner were to sue the makers of trivial copies, judgment would be for the defendants. The case would be dismissed because trivial copying is not an infringement.[195]

Three types of work are entitled to copyright protection. The first is a creative work, such as a novel. The second type of work is called derivative, because it is based on a preexisting work that has been recast, transformed, or adapted—such as a screenplay based on a novel. The third type of work entitled to copyright protection is a compiled work, such as Warren's Factbook. Copyrights in these three distinct works are known as creative, derivative, and compilation

---

194 See Nimmer 8.01.

195 Educational Testing Service v. Stanley H. Kaplan, Educational Center, Ltd., 965 F. Supp. 731, 736 (D. Md.1997).

copyrights. The Copyright Act has created a hierarchy in terms of the protection afforded to these different types of copyrights. A creative work is entitled to the most protection, followed by a derivative work, and finally by a compilation. This is why the Feist Court emphasized that the copyright protection in an actual compilation is "thin."[196]

Conclusion

Practice Tip: Here's the bottom line. If there is a lot of access, the songs may not have to sound identical to constitute copying. However, if there is very little access, then the similarity must be so great that basically the only thing that explains how you came up with the song is that you copied it. Most songwriters are also huge music fans who have likely listened to tons of music in their life, and some of it surely seeps into the songwriting. Prince had a rule that he would not listen to music while writing or recording a song, and this is a good idea.

---

196 Warren Publ. v. Microdos Data Corp., 115 F.3d 1509, 1515 n.16 (11th Cir.) (en banc), cert. denied, 522 U.S. 963, 118 S. Ct. 397, 139 L. Ed. 2d 311 (1997).

Chapter 26

● ● ●

DEFENSES TO MUSIC COPYRIGHT CASES

As an initial matter, you can argue the plaintiff has never registered the copyright or is not the lawful copyright owner. In addition to the usual common law defenses, listed from the most obvious to the more obscure: Plaintiff has no access to my song; there is no substantial or striking similarity; even if there's some similarity, it is not substantial, not protectable, not original, from a prior common source, in the public domain; and/or the defendant independently created their work. To defend against a copyright allegation, simply take all the things plaintiff must prove and say they have not met their burden. As the Bee Gees proved, if you do not get past the access prong, similarity will not be called into question.

Introduction and Limits of Fair Use

You can infringe on either the sound recording or the composition. Given the Bridgeport decision, there is no real defense to using a sample from a master recording, other than it was not from the master or it was a replay. Now, the recent Madonna decision is the majority view that recognized the defense of insubstantial use, which is a form of one of the factors of fair use.

While I discuss fair use here, it is important to note that there is very little case law where a defendant raises, let alone succeeds, in using a fair use defense for a replay or song infringement. That leaves the defenses of parody and no access or substantial similarity between the two songs.

Fair use can be a powerful defense—that's the good news. The bad news is that to assert it you must have been sued and the case is likely go to trial. Further, there's no "bright line" in most cases as to what is "fair use." Fair use started out as a common law defense, but has since been codified in Section 107. Fair use is just an allowed transformative use. For example, using portions of a copyrighted work in a commentary, criticism, or educational purpose of that work is generally allowed. Parody is also an allowed fair use, where you are making some commentary on the original work.

There is a four-part test to determine fair use:

1. Purpose of use (commercial or educational);
2. Nature of the copyrighted work;
3. Amount used and substantiality of the portion used in relation to the copyrighted work as a whole;
4. Effect of use on potential market of copyrighted work.

"Fair Use," like "substantial or striking similarity," is rather nebulous. Court case with specific facts need to flesh out "fair use":

> The Copyright Act provides an explicit exception to the copyright owner's exclusive rights: "the fair use of a copyrighted work . . . is not an infringement of copyright." 17 U.S.C. § 107. Fair use is an equitable rule of reason that defies general definition. Sony Corp. of Am. v. Universal City Studios, Inc., 464 U.S. 417, 448, 78 L. Ed. 2d 574, 104 S. Ct. 774 (1984). Sundeman v. Seajay Soc'y, Inc., 142 F.3d 194, 202 (4th Cir. 1998). The Copyright Act offers four factors to guide the determination whether a particular use is fair: (1) the purpose and character of the use, including whether such use is of a commercial nature or is for nonprofit educational purposes; (2) the nature of the copyrighted work; (3) the amount and substantiality of the portion used in relation to the copyrighted work as a whole; and (4) the effect

of the use upon the potential market for or value of the copyrighted work. 17 U.S.C. § 107. These factors are not exclusive, nor may they be "treated in isolation, one from another. All are to be explored, and the results weighed together, in light of the purposes of copyright." Campbell v. Acuff-Rose Music, Inc., 510 U.S. 569, 578, 127 L. Ed. 2d 500, 114 S. Ct. 1164 (1994).[197]

The first factor is generally the most important in copyright cases. However, when dealing with music cases, it is the third factor that likely has the most influence. Creative works are more protected than a set of facts. In music, this does not come up often because there is not much of a musical equivalent to a set of facts. But, as noted in the prior chapter, songs based upon very common chords may not have as much protection because they are not particularly unique. Courts not only look to how much of a song you are using, but what part of a song you are taking from. Thus, if you take a main riff or hook from a song, that is likely not going to qualify as fair use, unless you fit under the narrow exception of parody.

The fourth factor includes taking a potential market away from the original song.[198] Acknowledging the prior songwriter is not going to help you in a fair use case. Although, if you are using something that is de minimis, it begs the question of using it all since the use is marginal.

Details of the Four Factors[199]

1. The purpose and character of the use, including whether such use is of a commercial nature or is for nonprofit educational purpose.

---

197 Lowry's 271 F.Supp.2d at 747-8.

198 Rogers v. Koons, 960 F.2d 301 (2d Cir. 1992) (a sculpture based on a photograph was not fair use because a potential market of a sculpture of the photograph existed). If the use is de minimis, then there is no fair use analysis. Sandoval v. New Line Cinema Corp.147 F.3d 215 (2d Cir. 1998) (use of copyrighted photos in the movie *Seven* was de minimis because photos' use was fleeting and out of focus).

199 An entire book could be written about fair use, and it is very fact-intensive. This is simply meant as an overview.

Thus, ask why are you taking another's work, what are you doing with it, and are you looking to make money from your end product that includes the taken work? Education, news and criticism are generally regarded as fair use.

I know some musicians give away their music, or use the "pay what you want model." The DJ Girl Talk does this. He uses hundreds of samples in any given album and does not get permission to do so. While this may be somewhat helpful in arguing fair use, I do not think it is foolproof. If you are just giving away your music and knowingly plagiarizing others' music, you may not be successful in arguing fair use since that does not seem very fair. Plus, artists like Girl Talk tour and perform live and make money off the samples used. Now, certainly DJs such as Girl Talk add much to the samples and there's an art to what they do, but giving away music is no guarantee that you will fit under fair use.

2. The nature of the copyrighted work that you are allegedly taking from: In other words, what kind of work are you taking from? Is it comprised of facts or is it a creative work? Is it published or unpublished? This factor usually does not weigh much in most cases; presumably, if something is not creative, it may not be afforded as much protection as a "creative" work.

3. The amount and substantiality of the portion used in relation to the copyrighted work as a whole: The amount (quantity) and substantiality (quality) of the portion used in relation to the copyrighted work as a whole (how much did you take and was it a core portion of the borrowed work)?

    This is a big factor and there may be misunderstandings here among musicians. There is no such thing as a "small enough" sample. There is no bright line rule that says you can use, say, five seconds of something before a violation occurs. If you use someone's sample and it is a major part of your song—like Vanilla Ice's use of Queen's "Under Pressure" in his song "Ice, Ice Baby"—you likely have no fair use argument. But, if you use a five-second sample in a several-minute long song, you may have a fair use defense.

Getting back to the DJ Girl Talk: The fact that he's such a serial sampler may actually help his fair use argument. I think he could legitimately argue that he does not use a large amount of any particular sample, and because he uses so many samples, no one is any more important that another one in relation to any particular song.

4. The effect of the use upon the potential market for or value of the copyrighted work: Will your work reduce the ability of the copyright owner of the taken work to market it, or to get the expected price for a license or sale of it that would have likely been obtained had your work not included the taken material? This is very hard for the alleged copyright victim to prove, and this prong is not used much. Again, Girl Talk could easily argue that his use of samples does little to hurt the original artist; indeed, he might say it could help.

In conclusion, "[t]he ultimate test of fair use . . . is whether the copyright law's goal of 'promot[ing] the Progress of Science and useful Arts' would be better served by allowing the use than by preventing it."[200] Accordingly, fair use permits reproduction of copyrighted work without the copyright owner's consent "for purposes such as criticism, comment, news reporting, teaching (including multiple copies for classroom use), scholarship, or research."[201] The list is not exhaustive, but merely illustrates the types of copying typically embraced by fair use.[202]

The "Weird Al" Section: Parody–a "Fair Use" Defense

I often get asked about the legality of what "Weird Al" Yankovic does. Weird Al, for those who do not know, takes the melodies of popular songs and changes the lyrics to something comical. Michael Jackson's "I'm Bad" becomes "I'm Fat;" Coolio's "Gangsta's Paradise" becomes "Amish Paradise."

200 Castle Rock Entm't, Inc. v. Carol Publ'g Grp., Inc., 150 F.3d 132, 141 (2d Cir.1998) (quoting U.S. Const., art. I, § 8, cl. 8).
201 17 U.S.C. 107.
202 Castle Rock Entm't, Inc., 150 F.3d at 141.

Clearly, he transforms the song's lyrics, so he would need permission from the songwriter/publisher for doing that. He could argue that the song is parody, as 2 Live Crew successfully did in their case, although I am not sure all his music would fit into that narrow fair use exception. The bottom line: He always gets permission and has never been sued.

Below is an excerpt from an NPR story about him. The story is several years old. http://www.npr.org/templates/story/story.php?storyId=5482774.

In a career spanning more than 25 years, pop-music parodist "Weird Al" Yankovic hasn't exactly ranked among the music business' fiercest iconoclasts: He doesn't release his song parodies without the consent of the artists being parodied, and he's rarely used the Internet as more than a tool to promote his projects and connect with his fans. But a music label's efforts to block a (relatively tame) parody of James Blunt's ubiquitous hit "You're Beautiful" has Yankovic fighting back publicly, and using his Web site as a tool to do so.

According to Yankovic, Blunt himself gave his blessing to a song called "You're Pitiful," which was to appear on Yankovic's now-finished but as-yet-unreleased new album. But after Yankovic finished recording the parody, Atlantic Records, Blunt's label, told Yankovic that he couldn't release "You're Pitiful." Though Yankovic has encountered resistance from artists before — after a miscommunication involving permissions, Coolio publicly objected to a released parody of "Gangsta's Paradise," while Prince has always turned down Yankovic's requests to parody his hits — he says this is the first time a label has stepped in to squash the release of one of his parodies. (Quote an Atlantic representative: "We have no comment on this matter.")

So how, exactly, does a music label have a say in whether one of its artists can be parodied?

"The legality in this case is somewhat moot," Yankovic writes when contacted via e-mail. "James Blunt could still let me put it on my album if he really wanted to, but he obviously doesn't want to alienate his own record company . . . and my label could release the parody without Atlantic's blessing, but they don't really want to go to war with another label over this. So really, it's more of a political matter than a legal matter."[203]

Of course, it's not hard to circulate a song these days, and Yankovic has helped that process along by making an MP3 of the track available for free download on his Web site. It may not appear on Yankovic's new album, but "You're Pitiful" will still swirl around in cyberspace long after Blunt's original recedes from memory.

"I have a long-standing history of respecting artists' wishes," Yankovic writes. "So if James Blunt himself were objecting, I wouldn't even offer my parody for free on my Web site. But since it's a bunch of suits — who are actually going against their own artist's wishes — I have absolutely no problem with it."

---

203 He is correct. The label owns the sound recording, but Weird Al only needs permission from the publisher or songwriter to do what he does.

Chapter 27

● ● ●

DAMAGES IN COPYRIGHT CASES

The Copyright Act states that the copyright owner who prevails in an infringement action "is entitled to recover the actual damages suffered by him or her as a result of the infringement, and any profits of the infringer that are attributable to the infringement. . . ."[204] Damages are awarded to compensate the copyright owner for losses from the infringement, and profits are awarded to prevent the infringer from unfairly benefiting from a wrongful act.[205] Under the current Act, it is clear that it is the copyright owner who may, at his discretion, elect to recover statutory damages instead of actual damages and profits.[206] Such election may be made at any time before final judgment is rendered.[207]

Practice Tip: As mentioned in Section One, if you fail to register your work prior to an infringement, you are stuck with actual damage, whereas if you do register your work, you can choose whichever is greater.

---

204 17 U.S.C. 504(b).
205 H.Rep. p. 161.
206 Agence France Presse v. Morel, 934 F. Supp. 2d 584, 589 (S.D.N.Y. 2013).
207 17 U.S.C. 504I(c)(1).

Actual Damages

The Copyright Act provides that, "in establishing the infringer's profits, the copyright owner is required to present proof only of the infringer's gross revenues, and the infringer is required to prove his or her deductible expenses . . . ."[208] Accordingly, "all gross revenue is presumed to be profit 'attributable to the infringement,' unless the infringer is able to demonstrate otherwise."[209]

Actual damages represent the extent to which infringement has injured or destroyed the market value of the copyrighted work at the time of infringement.[210] If the infringement has entirely destroyed the value of the work, the damages then equal the full value.[211]

The basic rule for computing injury to the market value of a copyrighted work arising from infringement is to inquire what revenue would have accrued to plaintiff but for the infringement.[212] The plaintiff has the burden "of establishing with reasonable probability the existence of a causal connection between defendant's infringement and loss of anticipated revenue."[213] Once the plaintiff has met this burden of showing a causal connection, or "but for" causality, "the burden then properly shifts to the infringer to show that this damage would have occurred had there been no taking of the copyrighted expression."[214]

If plaintiff's lost profits are less than defendant's actual profits, plaintiff may recover lost profits under the rubric of actual damages; the plaintiff may further recover the difference between the lost profits and defendant's actual profits under the rubric of defendant's profits.[215] A plaintiff may not recover both actual damages and lost profits because that would be double recovery.

---

208 17 U.S.C. 504(b).

209 Nelson-Salabes, Inc. v. Morningside Dev., LLC, 284 F.3d 505, 512 n.9 (4th Cir. 2002).

210 In Design v. K-Mart Apparel Corp., 13 F.3d 559, 563 (2d Cir. 1994)

211 Golding v. RKO Pictures, Inc., 35 Cal. 2d 690, 221 P.2d 95 (1950).

212 Cohen v. United States, 100 Fed. Cl. 461, 477 (2011) (Treatise quoted).

213 Key West Hand Print Fabrics, Inc. v. Serbin, Inc., 269 F. Supp. 605, 613 (S.D. Fla. 1965).

214 Banff Ltd. v. Express, Inc., 921 F. Supp.1065, 1068 (S.D.N.Y. 1995); Harper & Row, Publishers, Inc. v. Nation Enters., 471 U.S. 539, 567, 105 S. Ct. 2218, 85 L. Ed. 2d 588 (1985).

215 Taylor v. Meirick, 712 F.2d 1112 (7th Cir. 1983).

In music cases though, this would seem to be rare. More often than not, there would be little or no lost profit, and the best recovery would be actual damages via defendant's actual profits. For example, if a defendant infringed on a rather undiscovered song and had a huge hit with it, the plaintiff may have actually benefitted from the infringement in that it exposed their forgotten song. Thus, only defendant's ill-gotten gains would be the damages.

When losses to the copyright owner are difficult to quantify, it is better to look to defendant's profits. When the infringement produces no gain to the infringer, the circumstances are ripe for awarding statutory damages. However, failure to timely register the work sacrifices the ability to recover statutory damages. To the extent that all those circumstances coalesce, the specter arises from the copyright owner being unable to win any recovery at all—even if the infringer acted willfully and deliberately.

The defendant's burden under the apportionment provision of Section 504(b) is primarily to demonstrate the absence of a causal link between the infringement and all or part of the profits claimed by the plaintiff. Because the rebuttable presumption of causation represents a presumption as to both cause-in-fact and proximate cause, there are two avenues of attack available to a copyright defendant. First, the defendant can attempt to show that consumers would have purchased its product even without the infringing element. Alternatively, the defendant may show that the existence and amount of its profits are not the natural and probable consequences of the infringement alone, but are also the result of other factors which either add intrinsic value to the product or have independent promotional value.[216]

Statutory and Willful Damages

Statutory damages can range from not less than $750 to no more than $30,000, as the court or jury deem just.[217] If a plaintiff chooses actual damages, they

---

216 Data General Corp. v. Grumman Sys. Support Corp., 36 F.3d 1147, 1171, 1175 (1st Cir. 1994).
217 17 U.S.C. 504(c)(1).

cannot change their mind and elect statutory damages if they are not satisfied with the jury's award.[218]

Punitive damages are not allowed in copyright infringement cases; where the defendant's conduct is willful, there is the possibility of assessing damages up to $150,000 for willful copyright infringement. Here, though, "willfully" means with knowledge that the defendant's conduct constitutes copyright infringement.[219]

The Copyright Act provides that the court may order the impounding "of all copies or phonorecords claimed to have been made or used in violation of the exclusive right of the copyright owner."[220] Section 503(b) of the Copyright Act 1 provides that, as part of a final judgment or decree, the court "may" order the destruction "or other reasonable disposition," of "all copies or phonorecords found to have been made or used in violation of the copyright owner's exclusive rights, and of all plates, molds, matrices, masters, tapes, film negatives, or other articles by means of which such copies or phonorecords may be reproduced."

"Though it is not essential to a finding of liability under the Copyright Act, the question of whether a defendant's infringement was willful does have a significant bearing upon the potential damages to be awarded in connection with the violation."[221]

"Innocent" Infringer and Notice

The Copyright Act permits a court to reduce statutory damages to a mere $200 per infringed work if "the infringer sustains the burden of proving . . . that such infringer was not aware and had no reason to believe that [its] acts constituted an infringement of copyright."[222] An infringer cannot obtain the

---

218 Feltner v. Columbia Pictures Television, Inc., 523 U.S. 340, 347, 118 S. Ct. 1279, 140 L. Ed. 2d 438 (1998).

219 Zomba Enters., Inc. v. Panorama Records, Inc., 491 F.3d 574, 584 (6th Cir. 2007).

220 17 U.S.C. § 503(a)(1)(A)

221 Castle Rock Entertainment v. Carol Publishing Group, Inc., 959 F.Supp. 260, 266 (S.D.N.Y. 1997).

222 17 U.S.C. § 504(c)(2).

reduction, however, if a proper notice of copyright appears on the material allegedly infringed.[223]

If the defendant sustains the burden of proving that she was not aware and had no reason to believe that her acts constituted an infringement of copyright, and the court so finds, the court may reduce the applicable minimum. Therefore, defendant must sustain the burden of proving good faith.[224] Moreover, a defendant is entitled to the reduced minimum if he proves not only that his infringing conduct was made in a good faith belief of the innocence of his conduct, but also that he was reasonable in holding that good faith belief.[225]

Existence of the notice is important because it informs the public that the work is protected by copyright, identifies the copyright owner, and shows the year of first publication. Furthermore, in the event that a work is infringed, if a proper notice of copyright appears on the published copy or copies to which a defendant in a copyright infringement suit had access, then no weight shall be given to such a defendant's defense based on innocent infringement in mitigation of actual or statutory damages, except as provided in section 504(c)(2) of the Copyright Act.

Practice Tip: Always put a prominent notice of your copyright on both songs and albums in order to tell the world you created it and avoid someone claiming they did not know it was copyrighted. It also may help in finding willful copyright violation.

---

223 17 U.S.C. 401(d), 402(d); see also Matthew Bender & Co. v. West Publ'g Co., 240 F.3d 116, 123 (2d Cir. 2001).

224 H. Rep., p. 163. See Basic Books, Inc. v. Kinko's Graphics Corp., 758 F. Supp. 1522, 1544 (S.D.N.Y.1991).

225 Childress v. Taylor, 798 F. Supp. 981, 994 (S.D.N.Y. 1992).

Chapter 28

●　　●　　●

FAMOUS COPYRIGHT CASES

Overview

Generally, most copyright infringement cases have two interrelated things about them: The plaintiff usually goes after big names (maybe in hopes of a settlement) and/or when the defendant had a huge hit based on someone else's song (that's worth a lot of money). Sometimes the plaintiff-songwriter is unknown, maybe never got enough credit, or is as big a star as the defendant, and, though rare, a star in his or her own right.

Most copyright cases have little or no actual damages if a defendant's tune never took off. These types of cases are where statutory damages and attorney fees come into play. Plus, they give a potential plaintiff leverage in settlement because the threat of statutory damages and attorney fees is there.

There are many music copyright infringement cases, so this is not meant as a definitive listing, but rather some of the more famous and interesting cases. With that intro, let's see these concepts play out in some actual cases.

Bright Tunes Music Corp. v. Harrisongs Music Ltd., 420 F.Supp. 177 (S.N.Y. 1976), or "He's So Fine" by the Chiffons v. "My Sweet Lord" by George Harrison This is probably the most famous copyright case. Ronald Mack wrote "He's So Fine" and it was eventually recorded by the girl group, The Chiffons. Bright Tunes was the publisher, and, thus, the copyright holder. Mack died in 1963, shortly after the song became a hit.

George Harrison began writing "My Sweet Lord" in 1969, using two-chords while singing "Hallelujah." Harrison actually wrote the song and gave it to Billy Preston, who played keyboards on some of the later Beatle's work, to record first. The song emanated from some chord changes he was playing with and was inspired by the Edwin Hawkins Singers' song "Oh, Happy Day"—a song whose copyright had apparently expired. Phil Spector produced Harrison's song.

"My Sweet Lord" was a #1 hit in the U.S. for four weeks and was the lead single off Harrison's triple-album, *All Things Must Pass*, which came out in November 1970. He was sued the following February. Harrison was obviously reluctant to give up the royalties from such a huge hit, so he attempted to settle the case and buy Bright Tunes' catalog. However, they wanted him to give up the copyright, which he refused. The case did not go to trial until 1976.

Harrison admitted he had heard the Plaintiff's song before. In 1962-63, "He's So Fine" was #1 in U.S., and #12 in England. The two songs had very similar structures; motifs A and B, and the harmonies were the same. Further, they both had the same grace note (a unique musical note added as embellishment) which even Harrison's expert admitted was not common. The experts talked about notes for days, and Harrison thought maybe the Plaintiff owned the notes.

Writing a song is a very personal and unexplainable process at times. It is like catching lightning in a bottle. It is amusing to read the federal judge's comments on chord progressions, "vamping," and the "free flowing exchange of ideas." Songwriting is a process that's hard to explain, and Harrison could not remember how some notes came about.

The Bottom line: Harrison lost. The judge found the two songs "virtually identical" and "the same song with different words." The infringement violation was found to be unintentional, though. While Harrison lost the case, he got some creative revenge when he recorded a response to the saga called "This Song." It was released in 1976, the year of the verdict. Check out the lyrics on the web. They are quite cutting.

In a story too long to go into detail now, Harrison's post-Beatles manager was Allen Klein, the man who squeezed The Verve out of their song "Bittersweet Symphony." After Harrison did not renew his contract with

Klein, the embittered manager passed on sensitive information to Bright Tunes and then bought them out of receivership and attempted to collect the judgment. After many years of litigation, Harrison eventually owned "He's So Fine" and paid only a fraction of the damages.

Selle v. Brothers Gibb, 567 F.Supp. 1173 (N.Ill 1983) aff'd 741 F.2d 896 (7th Cir. 1984), or "Let It End" by Ronald Selle v. "How Deep Is Your Love" by the Bee Gees
The plaintiff was an antique dealer and a songwriter on the side. He wrote "Let It End"[226] in 1975, and performed it twice in Chicago. He sent it to 11 publishers, but eight returned it as unsolicited—a common thing for publishers to do. He registered it in D.C., which, as I keep saying, is important. When he heard "How Deep Is Your Love" from *Saturday Night Fever* off a neighbor's transistor radio, he thought he recognized the song as his.

More than half the notes in the two songs are the same and Maurice Gibb identified plaintiff's tune on the stand as his after eight bars. There was no evidence of access because the Bee Gees had recorded "Deep" in France during 1977. The plaintiff argued that because the songs were so similar, there must have been access.

Bottom line: The jury found for Selle, but their verdict was reversed on Bee Gees' motion for judgment NOV. The similarity in tunes does not mean the group had access to it. Plaintiff never proved access to the song, and, while there's a relationship between access and substantial similarity, there needs to be some evidence of access, even when the songs are extremely similar.

Fantasy, Inc. v. John C. Fogerty, 1995 U.S. Dist. Lexis 6197, aff'd 984 F.2d 1524 (9th Cir. 1993), or "Run Through the Jungle" by Creedence Clearwater Revival v. "The Old Man Down the Road" by John Fogerty
This is one of the oddest copyright cases ever, and was very acrimonious. Fogerty sold the publishing to "Jungle" and all his CCR work to Fantasy Records, his former label, to get out of a bad record deal. Because the publisher

---

226 You can find this song on YouTube, though the sound is not great.

owns the copyright, it is the party-in-interest. Fogerty would not play CCR songs in public for years to deny performance rights to Fantasy Records.

Fantasy Records owner Saul Van Zantz sued Fogerty for copyright infringement. Now, in almost all cases, a songwriter can rip himself off because they have the right to create a derivative work from their original work. That was not the case here. So, Fogerty took the stand with guitar in hand and pointed out differences between the two songs. You cannot get a better expert witness than this![227]

Bottom line: Fogerty won, as the court declared there was no infringement. In 1994, after years of court battles, the U.S. Supreme Court granted him attorney fees. This was after Zantz sued him for defamation over a couple of songs on his 1985 album Centerfield. In a fitting end, when Zantz sold his interest in Fantasy Records, Fogerty re-signed with Fantasy and gained back the rights to his CCR songs. While maybe an unusual example, this case illustrates the importance for a songwriter to retain all the rights to their songs.

Three Boys Music Corp. v. Bolton, 1996 U.S. Dist. Lexis 22960 (C.D. CA 1996) aff'd 212 F.3d 477 (9th Cir. 2000), or "Love Is a Wonderful Thing" by the Isley Brothers v. "Love Is a Wonderful Thing" by Michael Bolton
Song titles cannot be copyrighted because lots of songs have the same title (although if it is really unique you could get it trademarked). While there are more than 80 songs with this title, this fact certainly does not help Bolton's cause.

Bolton and his co-writer claimed there was no access in this case, but the plaintiffs had DJs, playlists, and a host of a local music TV show to prove otherwise. Bolton did not help himself in this regard when it was revealed that he introduced Ronald Isley in 1988 by saying, "this man needs no introduction. I know every song he's ever done." Ouch.

The phrasing and melody of the song title are nearly identical. Bolton wondered aloud on work tape recording in the studio if the song he wrote

---

227 Fogerty could not really deny he had access to the prior song either.

sounded too much like Marvin Gaye's "Some Kind of Wonderful." So, be careful what you say when the tape is running in the studio!

Bottom Line: Bolton and co-writer were found guilty of infringement, and they and their record label were levied $5.4 million in damages.

Robin Thicke, Pharrell Williams v. Bridgeport Music, Gaye Estate, Case No. CV13-6004 (Cent. Dist. CA) or "Blurred Lines" by Robin Thicke v. "Got to Give it Up" by Marvin Gaye

As Thicke's song "Blurred Lines" (co-written with Pharrell Williams) became a huge hit, rumors started circulating that it bore a huge resemblance to Marvin Gaye's "Got to Give It Up." Give a listen to both. Thicke's lawyers took the unusual step of suing the Gaye estate (and George Clinton for a song that I don't think sounds like "Blurred Lines") asking for a declaratory judgment stating the two songs are not substantially similar. While I do not think you can get a declaratory judgment for this fact-intensive issue, it is a moot point because the Gaye estate counter-sued, alleging copyright infringement in this and other Gaye songs.

While a jury found in favor of the Gaye Estate, this quote from Thicke about the song from GQ magazine prior to this whole controversy could not have helped:

> "Pharrell and I were in the studio and I told him that one of my favorite songs of all time was Marvin Gaye's 'Got to Give It Up.' I was like, 'Damn, we should make something like that, something with that groove.' Then he started playing a little something and we literally wrote the song in about a half hour and recorded it."

Randy Craig Wolfe Trust v. Led Zeppelin (and a host of others), filed May 31, 2014 (E. Dist. PA) or "Taurus" by Spirit v. "Stairway to Heaven" by Led Zeppelin.

Listen to Spirit's song "Taurus" for a minute until the guitar intro kicks in, and then listen to the opening of "Stairway to Heaven." It is worth noting that Zeppelin toured with Spirit in 1968, and Jimmy Page apparently took an interest in the guitar opening of "Taurus."

My first thought when I heard of this lawsuit was, 'what took them so long?' "Stairway" came out in 1971. There is a three-year statute of limitations for copyright actions that begins to run on the date of the last infringement. Now, that album is going to be re-issued, so maybe that is what plaintiffs will argue and they can only go back three years for damages.

In the summer of 2016 a jury found that Zeppelin did not commit copyright infringement. Two things are important to note. First, the guitar line in both songs is quite common and may have derived from a prior common source such as Bach, as Jimmy Page testified. Second, when Taurus registered their song, they only registered the sheet music, so the jury never heard the actual song, only re-creations based upon the sheet music.

Practice Tip: In a copyright infringement case, you may be stuck with what you registered, so register the actual song and sound recording, not the sheet music.[228]

Tom Petty's "I Won't Back Down" v. Sam Smith's "Stay with Me"

In a statement given to *Rolling Stone*, Sam Smith's representatives acknowledge the similarities between the songs and confirmed that "Stay with Me" is now co-credited to Tom Petty and Jeff Lynne. "Not previously familiar with the 1989 Petty/Lynne song, the writers of 'Stay with Me' listened to 'I Won't Back Down' and acknowledged the similarity," the statement read. "Although the likeness was a complete coincidence, all involved came to an immediate and amicable agreement in which Tom Petty and Jeff Lynne are now credited as co-writers of 'Stay with Me' along with Sam Smith, James Napier and William Phillips." I do not know how the writers of "Stay with Me" never heard the Lynne/Petty composition all these years.

Tom Petty was very gracious about the whole incident in a statement on his website. "About the Sam Smith thing. Let me say I have never had any hard feelings toward Sam. All my years of songwriting have shown me these

---

228 Not that a lot of people today transcribe their songs to sheet music. You can certainly copyright the sheet music to your songs, but only in addition to the song and the sound recording.

things can happen. Most times you catch it before it gets out the studio door but in this case, it got by. Sam's people were very understanding of our predicament and we easily came to an agreement. The word lawsuit was never even said and was never my intention. And no more was to be said about it. How it got out to the press is beyond Sam or myself. Sam did the right thing and I have thought no more about this. A musical accident no more no less. In these times, we live in this is hardly news. I wish Sam all the best for his ongoing career. Peace and love to all."

Back when Smith's smash single came out, many listeners drew comparisons between the two tracks. In a story on Medium, Ed Rex even noted that there were identical notes, chords, rhythms and pitches. Naturally, there's a video on YouTube comparing and joining the two songs together. "Stay with Me" has sold almost four million copies worldwide and was one of the biggest tracks of 2014. It won a Grammy for Record of the Year, though there's no word on whether Smith will share it.

Petty and Lynne will get 12.5% of the song's revenues, and this makes sense if you understand the publisher's and composer's share we talked about. Smith's publisher takes half of the song's revenue, so prior to this settlement, Smith and his two co-writers would split the other half. Now, they must divide their half in half, meaning Petty and Lynne split 25%.

Chapter 29

● ● ●

HOW SONGS ARE BUILT WHY SONGS SOUND ALIKE CONCLUSION

In addition to experts testifying that the songs sound alike, there is also the question of whether a reasonable person thinks these songs sound substantially similar. The more common a song structure and chords, the harder it may be to prove copyright infringement. It is wise to never say in the studio or to a friend that a song you have written sounds a lot like another tune. If you think that's the case, change some notes or chords. Courts have acknowledged that the bulk of popular music is drawing from the same well.

> In assessing this evidence, we are mindful of the limited number of notes and chords available to composers and the resulting fact that common themes frequently reappear in various compositions, especially in popular music. See Arnstein v. Edward B. Marks Music Corp., 82 F.2d 275, 277 (2d Cir.1936). Thus, striking similarity between pieces of popular music must extend beyond themes that could have been derived from a common source or themes that are so trite as to be likely to reappear in many compositions. See Selle v. Gibb, supra, 741 F.2d at 905.[229]

---

229 Gasie at 1068-9.

Why do a lot of songs sound alike?

All music is derivative. John Lennon once said, "it's not who you steal from, it's how you steal." Picasso supposedly said, "Good artists borrow, great artists steal." While this may be an exaggeration, songwriters, like all artists, are inspired by others' work. They are music fans themselves. Certainly, there's a fine line between inspiration and borrowing too much, but modern music itself is a derivation of blues, country, African chants, and rhythm and blues. This is how music and art advances.

I have heard and read many interviews with songwriters over the years where they admit they were inspired by another song, or heard some chords they liked and tweaked them (or not). Most songs are inspired by others and that is fine; there are only so many good-sounding chord changes and progressions

As Questlove tweeted about Thicke's suit, "Just because a song is derivative that doesn't mean it's plagiarized."

A ton of songs have the same three or four chords. Look up Axis of Awesome on YouTube for proof. Axis of Awesome is a group that has videos where they play the same chords and then sing well-known hit songs across many genres.

All music is formulaic. Chords are just a series of notes, usually played on a guitar or piano. Almost all songs are built around a series of chords. There are only 12 notes that can be sung, and in any given major or minor chord, only two or three notes can be sung. Considering only so many chords sound good in a certain order, and that you can only sing so many notes within those chords, then that limits what is sung in most pop/rock records.

Modern rock/pop has been around a while now.

"[Copyright infringement] happens quite often for . . . a lot of different reasons. One, there is just a large quantity of recorded music. And rock music as a genre is now well over 50 years old. The amount of originality you can have is starting to get limited."[230]

---

230 Timothy English, author of Sounds Like Teen Spirit, to NPR. Search NPR for full story.

Ways to avoid being sued for copyright infringement:

1. Do not accept unsolicited material or listen to it.
2. Do not listen to music for a while prior to recording a song.
3. Be aware when you are inspired by another song, and make your new song different enough.
4. If you are cribbing another's chords, change a few.
5. Never tell anyone or say in a studio with tape running, "Boy, 'My Song' sounds a lot like 'This Song.'"

Conclusion

I have practiced law for more than 25 years in a variety of areas and this area of the law is by far the most interesting and fluid of them all. I write songs and have a love for music and I hope that has come across in this book. As the law in this area develops, and it surely will as it tries to catch up with technology, I will update this book as needed. There is always something to add and update, so the need for this will never go out of style. I hope you have learned something and have enjoyed reading this.

Keep on rocking!
© 2016 Jim Jesse

Made in the USA
Columbia, SC
14 January 2018